Lordly Cartoons

Lordly Cartoons

Alan Mumford

BURKE'S PEERAGE & GENTRY

This edition first published in Great Britain in 2003
by Burke's Peerage and Gentry (UK) Ltd

ISBN 0-9711966-1-3

British Library Cataloguing in Publication Data
A CIP catalogue record for this book can be obtained
from the British Library

Typeset & design by Land & Unwin, Bugbrooke
Printed and bound in Great Britain by CharterGroup,
Northampton & Lutterworth

Contents

Publisher's Foreword

The Burke family established a strong tradition of publishing less than flattering tracts and anecdotes about great landed families during the 19th and early 20th centuries. They presumably found the temptation arising from the intelligence they gathered for their *Peerage* and *Landed Gentry* volumes irresistible. It is a tradition we are delighted and proud to reassert in 2003 to coincide with our publication of the 107th hard copy edition of *Burke's Peerage Baronetage & Knightage*.

There are more than a few in society even today who automatically characterise all Lords as figures for ridicule. Lord Baker of Dorking suggests it is perhaps pervasive in his Introduction here. They normally do so in order to advance a populist cause based on the unproven hypothesis that democratic power exercised through Commoners is a superior form of societal organization to one based on heredity or selection from amongst the contemporary generation. They make no attempt to assess the work of the House of Lords as an Upper Chamber in Parliament since the Lords' insistence on Magna Carta and their long standing role as a counterbalance to the more transient Commoners, or to evaluate the myriad activities in which Lords engage by virtue of their inheritance including their leading role in local communities. But their populist bubbles can be burst! John Howard, in his masterly conduct of the *2000 Referendum on the Abolition of the Australian Monarchy*, showed how ill conceived the alternatives proposed there truly were. Tony Blair's New Labour zealots currently pursuing 21st century reform of the House of Lords in the United Kingdom have equally demonstrated how vacuous most of their alternatives are. Both reformist campaigns failed to realize that what works seldom needs fixing, and if a

time comes when it does not work … the requisite alternative can be expected to emerge. Lloyd George and Asquith with a few subsequent amendments got it about right in 1911.

Accordingly, it is important that in publishing this fine collection of cartoons we at *Burke's* loudly proclaim that we do so without any malicious intent. Despite generations of cartoon ridicule, everyone still 'loves a Lord'. We firmly belong to the school that believes laughing, with others, at yourself is one of the vital routes to real understanding of what works and what needs fixing. Acceptance and enjoyment of such humour is a sincere mark of respect for the creativity of the wits and wags who craft it. Many a true word is spoken in jest; many an honest opinion is forever captured in a cartoon. As such, we are especially glad that Dr Alan Mumford reminds us in Chapter 1 that the cartoons included show only '*selected* aspects of lordly history'. They indeed give a very lop sided impression of the nation's Lords focusing solely on those aspects that are fine targets for the cartoonist.

I would conclude by saying how profoundly grateful we are to Dr Alan Mumford for the very substantial research and scholarship he has been willing to bring to his task as author and editor here. It is his second such work carried forward since his nominal retirement from a lifelong career as a distinguished human resource management professional and teacher. It has given him enjoyable scope to advance his longstanding fascination with all things historical as well as his obsession with the collection of cartoons – which he of course shares with Lord Baker.

It was my own great pleasure to work with Dr Alan Mumford during his professional career for more than 20 years and everything we knew of him from that time and from the quality of his earlier cartoon title, *Stabbed in the Front: Post War General Elections through Political Cartoons*, implied he would be the perfect colleague here and made him the obvious choice. The moment I invited him at The Reform Club to undertake this work he agreed, and he has found the time not only to make an excellent job of it but also to meet our demands that its publication should be synchronized with the new 107th edition of *Burke's Peerage Baronetage and Knightage*.

Dr Gordon Prestoungrange
Baron of Prestoungrange
August 2003

Drawn to the Other Place

John Jensen

A cartoonist's view of the Lords is only partly governed by his (or her) politics. Environment plays its part, too. A fourth generation Australian like me, born in 1930, brought up while the Empire still flourished and the world map glowed pink, was taught an English history in which the negative aspects were erased, in tandem with an Australian history from which the iniquity – such as the annihilation of the native Tasmanians – had been expunged. This was a world of heroes, mostly sporting, untainted by gossip and fawned upon by an uncritical Press.

As a consequence, when I travelled to England in 1949 I was bloated with patriotic beliefs. England was 'home' and King George Vl reigned: the impressive stateliness of majesty had not yet been devalued, or debunked, by social and political change and an aggressively inquisitive media. My attitude towards the Lords, when I thought of them at all, was one of benign humour, this the patronising arrogance of a visiting nobody. On ceremonial occasions, dressed in their robes, furs and bauble coronets, the Lords, some-times herded together like sheep within the confines of Westminster Abbey, brought colour, pageantry, pomp and, occasionally, gossipy circumstances to the Nation's attention. In the Upper Chamber, in mufti, their thin voices debated whilst those around nodded or slept. Yet, innately conservative as they were, and are, by nature, they could rise above the fray of party politics. They acted like (fairly) serene grandparents keeping an eye on the brats brawling below. Even Labour or Conservative placemen, once they have been awarded peerages begin to speak and think and act like hereditary peers.

After living for more than fifty years in Britain, and now carrying a British Passport, my view of the House of Lords, and of the Royals, has altered less radically than I might have expected – except in viewing Australia's relationship with the Monarchy. Now that my homeland's future is turned towards Asia (and for other reasons not relevant here) I would be a republican if I still lived there. Here in Britain I have become a fence-sitter. Britain's old ruling-class may be *démodé* but our jealously guarded parliamentary democracy also suffers the disadvantages of its virtues. Anyone who has sat on a committee and tried to get things done will have encountered its exasperating downside. Committees postpone decisions, make bad judgements and find the finances disappointing: just like the House of Commons. The late George Lansbury (1859–1940), a democrat down to his Labour marrow, once uttered the heresy – in print, too! – that the best committee is a one-man committee. However, whatever the future, whether there is no-change, or all-change, or just the usual muddle through, all that happens will be grist to the cartoonist's mill, whatever his own politics might be.

If Lords are ever to be elected I pray that huge numbers of 'extinct volcanoes' will get the votes and that Members will continue to argue with their unique combination of eccentricity and common-sense. Let them wear ermine, let the smell of mothballs fill Westminster Abbey 'til our eyes water and may all their scandals be riveting. And, while I'm at it, let Royalty remain, roughly speaking, where it is. The removal of that Institution would simply replace one excellent subject for satire with another; one less picturesque and, from the taxpayers point of view, almost certainly more expensive. As a cartoonist I don't care, one way or the other, what happens. As a taxpayer, I do.

An elected breed of Lords would certainly be accountable to the electorate but, as any voter will acknowledge, accountability is a slow, uncertain process. Whereas today, faulty though the old system is, a Lord emeshed in scandal – Lord Archer, for example – is subject to the speedier attentions of an aggressive media bent upon forcing accountability. Yet cartoonists can take inspiration from a bumbling accountability just as easily as they can take inspiration from things as they are!

However, the Commons, not the Lords, is where the action is. There are, usually, few reasons to caricature the Lords, particularly the hereditary peers who by-and-large keep their heads below the parapet. This is a pity for some of them are beguiling subjects. On the other hand, after years of providing cartoon fodder in the Commons, wonderful subjects suddenly disappear to Another Place. Fortunately, in small compensation, a few hardy Peers descend to the Lower Chamber for a brief gambol in the spotlight before again finding themselves Upstairs. A few treasured subjects, moving in both directions, come to mind:

Lord Stansgate (1925–) transmogrifying backwards into Tony Benn in 1963 was a welcome, staring-eyed vision (in his early days) on any cartoonist's drawing board. Such a pity it wasn't (and still isn't) possible to translate his unusual speech – reminiscent of a smoker sucking on a wet briar pipe – into cartoon form.

Even more drawable was Lord Hailsham (1907–2001) who renounced his peerage in 1963, became Quintin Hogg, and was later climbed upstairs again, in 1970, as Lord Hailsham of Marylebone. He was a distinguished, occasionally irreverent, Lord Chancellor. As a subject for caricature he required little exaggeration. Someone once remarked that he had the face of a battered cherub – at least, I think it was said of Hailsham; if it wasn't it should have been. Even his clothes were a delight to sketch: the too short trousers; the seemingly huge turnups, and, while bicycling his way to the Woolsack, the bicycle clips. His rage – on television, reviling John Profumo during the Profumo scandal – reminded me of a child's tantrum. His ringing of a handbell as a rallying symbol at the Conservative Party

Conference in 1957 was a further example of his irrepressibility, as was his comment (quoted by Greg Knight in his compilation of political invective, *Parliamentary Sauce*.) 'Sitting on the Woolsack in the House of Lords is very boring, so I used to sit there as little as possible and amused myself by saying "bollocks" to the Bishops.' In spite of which, Hailsham was that rare thing in politics, an intellectual.

I'm not sure where Lord Longford (1905–2001) should be placed intellectually. His prison visits, particularly to the Moors murderer Myra Hindley, raised eyebrows, but a much publicised visit to Denmark, to see what Porn was *really* about – as part of a doomed anti-pornography crusade – was a cause of prolonged ribaldry nationwide. Lord Longford, accompanied by a retinue of braying journalists, set out on an earnest quest for the bare facts, which he soon found in abundance. Cartoonists couldn't believe their good fortune! Years later, in a Press interview, Longford admitted that yes, he had been affected by what he had seen. Unfortunately, he didn't elaborate on this

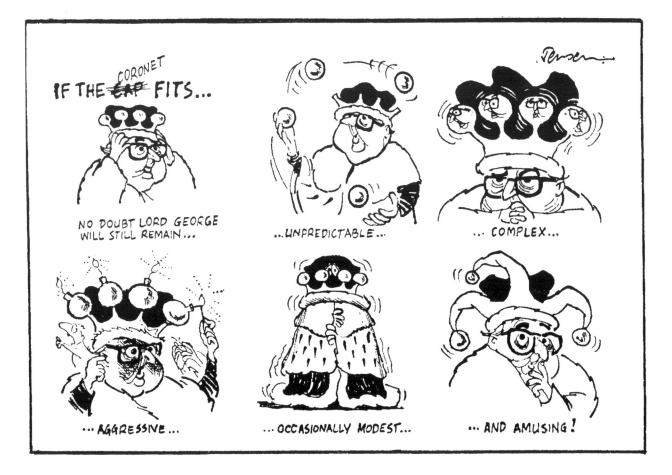

modest and, for journalists totally inadequate, confession.

The elevation of George Brown, Lord George-Brown (1914–1985) removed a wonderfully warm, fallible politician from the caricaturist's grasp. He, who had held many distinguished Posts in Government, including the deputy leadership of the Labour Party, and who lusted after the Premiership, drank little, but that little was too much. He simply couldn't hold his liquor. His tragedy was that he enjoyed it so much. Cartoonists took pictorial advantage of him but were generally sympathetic. Today, the Press would bay for his blood.

Sir Alec Douglas Home (1903–1995) was chalk to Baron George-Brown's cheese. He disclaimed his peerage in 1963 and, probably to his relief, was created a Life Peer in 1974. Sandwiched in-between were eleven hectic years in the Commons. He wore around his thin body an old-fashioned air of 'sang-froid habituel'. His pale, skeletal face sported not only a tight upper lip but also a tight lower lip; his lips barely moved when he spoke. I was sometimes reminded of strange characters in Hammer films (see Chapter 6). His other gift

to cartooning – particularly to Vicky of the *Evening Standard*, and the *New Statesman* – was his box of matches, these because he was no good at sums and they helped him, so he said, to understand how the Budget added up.

Vicky, unwittingly, also helped rather than hindered the Prime Ministership of Harold Macmillan, Earl of Stockton (1894–1986) whose politics he despised. Vicky tried to cut Macmillan down to size by drawing him, ironically, as Superman. Instead of being diminished by this portrayal, Macmillan to Vicky's chagrin, seemed to thrive. I drew Macmillan many times while he was Prime Minister, always with pleasure (the pleasure arose from his caricaturable face rather than from his politics, although those were caricaturable, too) but rarely after his elevation. Once, when he was very old and frail, I borrowed Vicky's Superman gear but added the Earl's cardigan, and made what I thought was a sad, poignant caricature, yet when it was published I was accused, by Conservatives, of callous insensitivity.

The House of Lords usually, though not invariably, ushers its members into obscurity whether they want it or not. This is an

unfairness for which the cartoonist, eager for any subject on which to lay his venom, finds hard to forgive.

John Jensen was political cartoonist of the *London Sunday Telegraph* 1961–79, and for the entire run of *NOW!* magazine, 1979–81. During the 70's he was social cartoonist of the *Spectator* and theatre caricaturist of the *Tatler* magazine. He has illustrated around 70 books and for many years drew regularly for *Punch*. He is founder member and former Chairman of the British Cartoonists' Association and a founder member and former Chairman of the Cartoon Art Trust. In 2002 he held a retrospective exhibition to celebrate fifty-five years as a cartoonist and in the same year was presented with a Lifetime Achievement Award by the Nottingham Cartoon Festival.

Introduction
The Rt Hon Lord Baker of Dorking CH PC

The history of the Peerage is a history of decline. The Lords were most powerful in feudal times when their power derived from the land they had acquired through war, the knights and soldiers they could raise from it, and the taxes they could extract from their subjects. The King was the first among equals but over the centuries the power of the monarchy held them in check until the trading merchant classes established their own position which was consolidated through the constitutional upheaval of the 17th Century that saw the authority of the House of Commons firmly established.

In the 18th Century the great aristocratic families retained their political position by influencing the choice of MPs. But, even so, in that century 15 of the King's first ministers came from the House of Lords. In the 19th Century there were 12 Prime Ministers from the House of Lords, but in the 20th Century only one – and that was right at the beginning for just one year. The power of the Lords, as Alan Mumford so clearly charts, has been constrained and is curtailed, resulting in the 20th century in a great constitutional battle.

In spite of this, Lords, both great and small, enjoyed a prestigious social position and they diverted themselves in many ways: some were gifted amateur scholars; patrons of artists and architects; leaders of fashion; racehorse owners; and bon viveurs.

In this delightful and amusing book Alan Mumford finds many prints and cartoons that depict the role of the Lords. But while only a few managed to get a seat at the high table of politics, some were close enough to persuade the world that they really mattered. The irreverence of the political cartoons in the late 18th and early 19th Centuries skewered individuals and undermined their assumed natural authority. In *Punch* they became figures of fun, emerging from the backwoods with rod and gun, wearing eccentric clothes, and with disconcerting habits.

Cartoonists love a Lord – the symbols were so easy: ermine, coronets and castles. These symbols were soon transformed from points of recognition to ridicule. As many were rich and time hung heavy upon their hands, some Lords took to gambling, partying on a grand scale, and some went bankrupt. The barbs of the cartoonists struck home and drew blood. It was, of course, the very bluest blood. They ceased to be figures of respect and became figures of fun. They were an easy target for Lloyd George.

Kenneth Baker by KAL

The Author

Alan Mumford is an expert practitioner and author in
developing managers. He has an extensive collection
of books and original political cartoons. This is
his second compilation of cartoons, following
*Stabbed in the Front: Post War General Elections
through Political Cartoons*.

Selected Aspects of Lordly History

Origins and Titles

Historians are unable to pinpoint exactly the date on which either the titles of 'Lords' and 'Ladies', or the formal existence of a House of Lords commenced. For the purposes of this book the relevant history starts in 1746 with the first cartoon included here, that of Lord Lovat, who was tried and executed in 1745 for rallying the Highland clans on behalf of the Pretender in 1745. Although unique in being executed, he can be seen as one of the long line of Lords who in one situation or another have attempted to act like King Canute in trying to turn back the tide of history.

As with many other aspects of British society and constitutional practice the descriptions Lord or Lady, and the institution of the House of Lords are confusing because not coterminous. Wives of Knights and Baronets are called Lady; not all Lords are members of the House of Lords, and not all members of the House of Lords are Lords; at the time of writing a number of Bishops remain. The generic title 'Lord' in this book has most often been used here. (Cartoonists have to avoid an important potential solecism – Marquises and Dukes are addressed as 'Your Grace' not 'My Lord'.)

Politics and Lords

The political role of the House of Lords, and of individual Lords, provides a major focus. Until 1834 and the passage of the Great Reform Act (vigorously opposed and indeed rejected twice by the House of Lords) the Commons and Lords were broadly seen to be of equal political significance. Wellington's contribution to the eventual passage of that Bill, by withdrawing himself and one hundred of his fellow Peers from the vote, may be seen as almost equal in its effect upon British society as his defeat of Napoleon seventeen years earlier.

The increased credibility and therefore power of the House of Commons was set then and further encouraged by successive Reform Bills about which the House of Lords usually complained, but which it did not veto. It was prepared to emasculate or veto other Bills, perhaps most significantly attempts to introduce Irish Home Rule.

In 1909 the House of Lords faced a challenge deliberately contrived by David Lloyd George, the Liberal Chancellor of the Exchequer. He included in his Budget items which the majority in the House of Lords saw as being explicitly punitive in relation to themselves (especially what we would now see as a tiny increase in Death Duties). The convention, though not of course a written constitutional requirement, had been that the Lords did not reject 'Money Bills'. The struggle which occurred when they did so produced hundreds of cartoons to accompany the major constitutional crisis. A combination of good sense and terror at the thought of their membership being overwhelmed by the addition of five hundred specially created peers caused the House of Lords eventually to pass the Budget. They also felt obliged to pass the Parliament Act of 1911 which circumscribed their powers. They were given only the power of one month delay for any 'Money Bill', and in effect a two year delay on any other Bill sent to them by the House of Commons. In 1949 that provision was reduced in effect to one year.

At the time of the furore over the Lloyd George Budget, the Lords' rejection of it and discussion on the Parliament Act, major reform of the House of Lords was for the first time seriously on the political agenda. (Winston Churchill in his Liberal phase had argued beforehand for major reform.)

Although the preamble to the 1911 Act, and discussion around it had stated that this was only the first measure to produce a more effective political balance between the House of Commons and the House of Lords, and not a permanent solution, no successful legislation was actually passed to reform the membership of the House of Lords until the Labour Government in 1999. Even then the resolution was only partial in the sense that the vast majority of hereditary peers were removed from the House of Lords; the way in which the membership of a second or re-titled chamber and its powers should be established remained unresolved.

The most significant event politically between the 1911 Act and the 1999 Act was not the further reduction in powers for the Lords in 1949, but the introduction by a Conservative Government under Harold Macmillan of Life Peerages in 1958. This was intended to provide a wider range of contribution within the second chamber, but since it also gave additional credibility to the House of Lords the arrangement was opposed by the Labour Party. However it eventually took advantage of the capacity to nominate life peers – an arrangement which left the Lords with a majority which more frequently opposed Labour legislation that it did that of any Conservative Government. (Arthur Balfour as Leader of the Conservative Opposition in 1906 had implied the House of Lords would always ensure that Unionist policies prevailed – thus the description of the Lords as 'Mr. Balfour's poodle' by Lloyd George in 1908.)

Disclaiming a Peerage

Not all eldest sons of peers, or all those who became peers actually wanted to acquire their title. The 2nd Viscount Astor attempted to get a Bill passed in 1919 when an M.P. which would have enabled him to avoid succeeding his father. The real struggle occurred however when Anthony Wedgwood Benn, as he was then called, succeeded his father as Lord Stansgate in 1960. Benn fought a long battle, not originally particularly encouraged by his colleagues in the Labour Party, which led to the Act of 1963 which enabled individuals who succeeded to a peerage to 'disclaim' it.

Benn did so immediately. The facility was subsequently used in 1963 by Lord Hailsham and Lord Home in order to make more credible their claims to succeed Harold Macmillan as Prime Minister.

Disclaimers for Benn, Home and Hailsham were necessary because while there had been 28 Prime Ministers who were members of the House of Lords, there had been no lordly Prime Minister since the Marquis of Salisbury in 1902. Stanley Baldwin had been preferred to Viscount Curzon in 1922, in part because Curzon was in the Lords. Viscount Halifax in 1940 made no serious effort to succeed Neville Chamberlain partly through a modest though accurate assessment of his own capacity, partly because he did not believe he could operate as Prime Minister from the Lords.

Elevation to a Peerage

Lloyd George in the course of his battles with the Lords in 1909 had talked about 'a body of 500 men chosen at random from amongst the unemployed.' While this was a splendid example of political invective, it was in no sense fully true of the composition of the House of Lords at that time. Although originally composed of people owning large amounts of land, it had gradually become a home for rewarding successful politicians (Cecils under Elizabeth), male companions and individuals prepared to pay for peerages (James I). The Royal mistresses of Charles I had also been given titles though not seats in the House. By the 19th Century these traditional methods of entry were increasingly supplemented by individuals whose main claim was acquired through commerce and industry. Public benevolence of a general kind had been complemented by contributions to political parties and by the 1890s by a direct association between a contribution and a peerage. Lloyd George, as we will see in the relevant chapter, took the process of enabling individuals to purchase peerages to its most extreme – his final expression of contempt for peerages.

While the great aristocratic titles continued their association with the land, with exceptions such as the Dukes of Westminster, it was no longer the prime source of wealth and power. While public benevolence remained a feature for a considerable proportion, and work for charities gave explanation for some ennoblements, the continuing association of peerages and services rendered in a less benevolent sense continued. Of particular significance for this book has been the willingness of Prime Ministers to propose and Monarchs to agree peerages for owners of the press. Only Rupert Murdoch of the great newspaper owners has not been ennobled. He preferred to place himself in the United States.

Peerages have also been rewards for politicians – in some cases recognising extraordinarily high achievement, in others merely devoted if occasionally shadowy service within a political party. In the first category are Earldoms for Balfour, Baldwin, Lloyd George, Attlee and Eden, and (late in his life) Macmillan. While life peerages continue to flow for subsequent Prime Ministers who have chosen to accept them – Wilson, Callaghan, and Thatcher – hereditary titles have been almost entirely in abeyance since 1958 and the introduction of life peerages. Margaret Thatcher, characteristically taking her own line, gave hereditary peerages to Whitelaw and George Thomas who were childless. Macmillan was awarded the hereditary Earldom of Stockton presumably as an ex-prime ministerial entitlement. Otherwise only royals – e.g. York and Wessex – have been ennobled.

Not all Prime Ministers acquired peerages. Queen Victoria did not offer one to Gladstone, claiming she knew he would not accept it. Campbell Bannerman, Bonar Law, Chamberlain, and MacDonald perhaps were prevented by illness. Edward Heath and John Major so far have chosen not to accept peerages. The most glittering exception is Winston Churchill. In his case he was offered a Dukedom on his retirement – but only when the Queen had been reassured that he would not accept it. Three Labour Prime Ministers have accepted peerages. We know which Labour people have accepted peerages, but know little of those who have refused them, except memorably R H Tawney who when offered a peerage by Ramsay MacDonald asked 'What harm have I ever done to the Labour Party?'

The political aspect of Lords has inevitably provided a major focus for this book because that is what has placed most of them in the public eye in the last two centuries. Earlier, before cartoons appeared, their significance arose from land and the wealth that arose from it. Land was the basis of power – castles – and conspicuous consumption – stately homes. The quiet work of public benevolence that many have and continue to donate to the well-being of British society is not recognised here, because it provides no exciting issues for cartoonists to portray. The role of some of them outside politics is identified in cartoons because of what they have done in industry, commerce, finance, culture and sport. Some have added to the gaiety of the nation, at cost to themselves and their families, by being involved in scandals, sometimes within and sometimes outside politics. At an extreme from scandals, some have given great intellectual sustenance to our country. Others, through opening their 'stately homes' to the public have provided an insight into the kind of lives led by very rich people before they invested their money in less conspicuous consumption.

Inclusions and Exclusions

In nearly all cases, the personalities included here are the holders of the full peerage rather than those who had a subsidiary title as a son or daughter of a peer. Where this rule might have led to the exclusion of some really interesting cartoons, it has been broken. The other exclusions have been of legitimate successors in the royal line, on the grounds that they are seen by most of us as being royal rather than lordly.

2

Cartoons and Caricature in The United Kingdom

Origins and Meanings

Drawings exaggerating particular features of individuals existed, particularly in Continental Europe, before they were introduced in the UK by George Townshend's caricatures of politicians in the middle of the Eighteenth Century. The original use of the word 'caricature', derived from the Italian word *'caricatura'* to describe an exaggerated portrait, began its appearance then as defining a depiction of an individual.

It is an extraordinary coincidence in a book about cartoons of Lords that the first significant caricaturist was himself a Viscount, later a Marquis (see page 13 for a Townshend caricature). William Hogarth, the first in the great run of British caricaturists, actually disliked both the word and many of the physical expressions of it. His later successors, with the exception of Max Beerbohm, have generally described themselves as cartoonists. So we are faced with a question, as to whether there is any difference in what actually appears which differentiates caricatures from cartoons – and where and when the term 'cartoon' appeared.

The second question is the easier to answer. Preliminary drawings for works of art had been called cartoons for centuries – see Leonardo and Michelangelo. In the United Kingdom, the word 'cartoon' was given prominence by the competition held to design buildings for a new Houses of Parliament in 1843. These preliminary drawings were called cartoons. The term was taken up by the magazine *Punch* founded in 1841. In 1843 John Leech in *Punch* satirised an exhibition of those cartoons for decorations for the new Houses of Parliament: he drew cartoons of the cartoons.

While there is still some tendency to call single person images caricatures the word cartoon has essentially taken over as the general description for a drawing aimed at portraying both individuals and collections of people in social or political cartoons.

What sort of portrayal?

For this book we can put aside 'joke' cartoons, in which the purpose of the cartoon is essentially to deliver a supportive pictorial representation to the main point of the cartoon which is the caption. *Punch* was a main repository for such cartoons. One of the most famous depicted a scene in which the drawing had no particular significance, but the caption did; since it represented a curate claiming of his egg that 'parts of it are excellent'. In a very different milieu the cartoons of Donald MacGill, although sometimes depending to a degree on physical exaggeration of bodies, primarily depended upon the caption e.g. 'Has anyone seen my little Willie?'

It is difficult to be categoric in offering this definition of joke cartoons, since captions or the text included within those cartoons which are the prime subject of this book, may have on occasions as much significance as the drawing itself.

Consideration of 'joke' cartoons leads to a crucial feature of cartoons of the kind used here, whether the cartoon is primarily intended to raise a laugh or produce a wince. However even that differentiation creates problems not least because cartoonists differ in their beliefs and ways of portraying content in their cartoons. The history of cartoons in Britain from Hogarth to the present day shows significant differences in the overt intention of cartoonists, and especially at the end of the Twentieth Century and continuing now, an aggregation of cartoonists around a style which exaggerates physical characteristics.

Some of the drawings included here were seen by their originators as portraits. Hogarth himself objected to the word 'caricature' and would have hated to be described as a caricaturist, not least because although his prints had a significant social purpose he saw himself primarily as an artist and not as a cartoonist or caricaturist. (Topolski, see page 47, was also an artist rather than a caricaturist). Hogarth's portrayal of social situations – 'The Rake's Progress' and his 'Election' series – made a significant social point, but not in most cases through a major physical exaggeration. James Gillray, at the end of the 18th Century and the beginning of the 19th, moved into exactly this latter form of physical exaggeration. His Charles James Fox had eyebrows the like of which were not seen until cartoonists portrayed Denis Healey in the 20th Century. French Revolutionary figures were at least cadaverous, and often cannibalistic, in form. Gillray was very willing to use bodily functions of a most elemental nature to portray events and the activities of politicians. Other cartoonists (not then so called) such as Williams and Rowlandson also emphasised physical characteristics.

The exaggerated use of facial or bodily forms stopped as suddenly as it had started. The major cartoonist of the early Victorian age, H.B., drew relatively shadowy figures without sharp lines or the colours used by his predecessors. Politicians were recognised as often by the features around them as by their own facial features – except for the Duke of Wellington with his hooked nose. Wellington indeed provided the opportunity for the extension of an existing form of recognition in cartoons, by the use of his famous Wellington boot as an element in many cartoons. *Punch*, although created as an explicitly satirical magazine, followed the same decorous line. This is particularly evident in the long-running series by their main political cartoonist, Tenniel (who was, of course, also famous as the illustrator of the *Alice* books). Although Tenniel's portrayal of foreigners would nowadays be seen as often politically incorrect, his treatment of politicians at home was relatively gentle. His cartoons of Benjamin Disraeli, which would have left no reader in any doubt as to Tenniel's view of Disraeli's racial antecedents, were an exception (see page 17). Tenniel's successors on *Punch*, such as Linley Sambourne, Leonard Raven Hill, and finally Bernard Partridge who like Tenniel drew for *Punch* for fifty years continued essentially the same style of drawing. Physical exaggeration was not their form.

From the 1890s to the 1920s the most admired caricatures were those drawn by Max Beerbohm, whose fame and significance rests not on the location of their publication (small circulation magazines) but by the accuracy with which he pinned down some physical characteristics of individuals (although he was not a good draughtsman). In some ways Beerbohm's caricatures reverted to 18th Century form since, perhaps unsurprisingly in view of his literary skills, he included text in the cartoon which pointed up the subject.

The development of style and readership

Originally, cartoons published in prints reached a small readership. The newspaper revolution, and especially the popular press which provided opportunities for cartoonists, did not immediately produce a difference in style. This occurred with the arrival in this country of an Australian, Will Dyson, in 1909. In 1912 he became the first cartoonist for the Labour Party paper, *The Daily Herald*. Dyson was a critic of the Capitalist system happily ensconced in a paper which in those idealistic days believed in the potential for Socialism. Dyson was a clear supporter of the idea that cartoonists could draw with pens apparently dipped in vitriol (in the days when an educated public knew what vitriol was). His criticism was direct and savage; the physical forms he drew began to see the use of more exaggerated forms – the Capitalist who was literally bloated in form. His war cartoons gave a similarly savage treatment to our German enemies – though other popular cartoonists were of course also ready to engage in this.

Dyson's pre-eminence was brief – and for what was then a fairly small circulation newspaper. His successor in terms of the esteem accorded him both by contemporaries and in more recent times was David Low. Low also came here from Australia, although he was a New Zealander by birth. He shared nothing in style with Dyson, and was certainly not a Socialist despite the attempts of some of his victims to portray him as such. He was prepared to make fun of anybody – but the fact was that most of the governments from 1918–1939 were conservative in orientation, usually Conservative in composition – with brief interventions from Labour Governments who were also conservative but more confused. Amongst Low's extraordinary contribution to the art of the cartoon was the fact that he created three representational images as vehicles for expressing his ideas. Harry Furniss had caricatured Gladstone with a high collar – the collar getting larger over the period in which he portrayed him. But Gladstone's face was still there above the collar, just as Wellington was drawn with his boot. Low, in addition to his normal range of cartoons of people and events, created his three representational images which were a unique form of cartoon art. The first, through the double-headed ass, portrayed the Coalition Government after 1918. After a long period with no additional image, he produced Colonel Blimp through which he portrayed any self-satisfied and complacent institution or individual, and then the TUC carthorse representing a basically useful but slow animal. (Low's most significant contemporary was Strube on *The Daily Express* – his sole but important image was that of 'The Little Man' through whom Strube expressed questions, comment, and bewilderment.)

In addition Low produced, mainly for the *New Statesman*, what in his autobiography he called 'Portraits chargés' – but which the *New Statesman* called caricatures of individuals. Like his general cartoons, his caricatures were more subtly satirical than exaggerated in form. For example his Lloyd George showed him in puckish form, and Churchill in a relatively benign mood. Portraits of Asquith in his later days, and Lord Birkenhead especially, were much more revelatory (see page 26).

The emphasis given here to Low is due to the fact that he is still held in considerable reverence by most current cartoonists (as was exemplified at an exhibition of Low's work in Westminster Hall in 2002), and because more than any other cartoonist he set down in his various books and articles views about the nature and purpose of cartooning – on which more below.

Low was eventually succeeded on *The Evening Standard* (after an intervening period) by the explicitly Socialist and much angrier Vicky – yet another in the gallery of cartoonists from overseas (in this case of Hungarian Jewish parents from Berlin). The expression 'Spoonerism' derives from a grammatical mistake made consistently by an Oxford don, whose sole claim to fame is precisely that he gave his name to this particular mistake. Vicky's great importance and influence as a cartoonist has been partially spoiled by his one great mistake. This was to portray, as he planned satirically, Harold Macmillan as 'Supermac'. Unfortunately from his point of view the intention was not matched by the result, since it gave at least some readers the idea that Macmillan was exactly the Superman that Vicky was claiming him not to be (see Jensen earlier).

Vicky's cartoons were more overtly critical, more likely to exaggerate the physical form of his victims than the cartoons of Low. He was the first cartoonist of whose work I was really conscious as a reader. Sometimes you smiled, sometimes you applauded the direction of his shafts, and sometimes they caused you to jolt back mentally in surprise. Like Low, Vicky produced individual caricatures, especially for *The New Statesman*.

Political opponents were often sharply critical of Vicky's style as being unduly savage – a comment which would astonish many of us looking at cartoons today. Indeed the political bias in such comments is evident if you look at the cartoons of his most significant contemporaries, Cummings on *The Daily Express* and Illingworth in *The Daily Mail* (though Illingworth in Punch was on the whole not violently critical of individuals). Like Low, Cummings invented an image – Mr Rising Price – to illustrate what was seen in the 1940s and 1950s as damaging levels of inflation. These were of course in Cummings' mind largely the product of a Labour

Government, although the rising prices were trivial compared with those produced by later Conservative Governments.

Much more than Vicky, Cummings indicted his political opponents with cartoons which created an image of extreme beliefs. He created cartoons of Nye Bevan and Tony Benn – as a staring-eyed fanatic – which at least reinforced the many words written to assert that they were bitter Left-wing quasi-revolutionaries. In contrast his images of Margaret Thatcher portrayed her as a sweet faced blonde whose strong views were expressed through captions, not exaggeration of her facial features.

Just as the poet Philip Larkin was wrong about the date on which sex was supposed to have started in the UK, some commentators are wrong in supposing that savage cartoons started with Ralph Steadman and Gerald Scarfe in the 1960s. What these cartoonists and successors such as Steve Bell and Martin Rowson have developed is a style in which physical exaggeration has become a major aspect of the cartoon in a way which was not true for Vicky and Low, let alone 19th Century predecessors. Connections can be seen to the violence of some of Gillray's cartoons. Without exhaustive biographies we cannot know the extent to which the ferocity of views they express are caused by their personal political anger, or by their pref-erence for a particular style of cartooning.

It may be thought that the difference from one cartoonist compared with another is a matter of preferring wit to a razor slash in terms of the treatment offered. Do you prefer the wit involved in Low's portrayal of J.H. Thomas as The Rt. Hon. Dress Suit, or Bell's portrayal of the second President Bush with monkey feet?

Some cartoonists seem to have taken the view of Cromwell's injunction to the artist painting his portrait, that he should be portrayed 'warts and all'. But then this does not apply only to cartoonists; as was seen with Graham Sutherland's portraits of Somerset Maugham and Winston Churchill. Notoriously Lady Churchill destroyed Sutherland's portrait of Churchill – though perhaps she would have wanted to do the same to cartoons drawn by Illingworth for

Punch and Scarfe for *Private Eye* on the aged Churchill.

In a political context it is intriguing that whereas 19th Century politicians used flamboyant language about each other – Disraeli on Gladstone: 'a sophistical rhetorician inebriated with the exuberance of his own verbosity' – while cartoons were moderate in content and style, the reverse has happened in our own time. We no longer even have the equivalent of Lloyd George 'an aristocracy is like a cheese: the older it is the higher it becomes' or Aneurin Bevan on the Conservative Party – 'lower than vermin'. Yet many modern day cartoonists employ the rhetoric and exaggeration that politicians themselves no longer use.

The Cultural Background

The *Punch* cartoons of Tenniel were often deferential, or even reverential, rather than sharply critical when it came to portraying, for example, Queen Victoria or the British Lion. Queen Victoria would have had no reason to be upset by Tenniel's cartoons of her – though her descendants have every right to be upset about how they are portrayed now.

In the 18th and 19th Centuries it would be unlikely that any major political speech would omit some classical reference to Greek or Latin texts. Quotations both assumed that support from classical history aided the point being made and also that the quotation would be understood because it was addressed normally in the Houses of Parliament to people who had been through the same classical education. Cartoonists addressing a wider audience and perhaps themselves not necessarily well-versed in classical literature were less inclined to use Greek or Latin and more inclined to use references from the Bible, from Shakespeare and, later, from Dickens. They would also base their cartoons sometimes upon familiar works of art such as Millais' 'Bubbles', and Holman Hunt's 'The Scapegoat'.

I have invented a word 'referential' to describe these cartoons. They seem to me to combine both reference back to familiar texts or drawings, and also reverence in the sense of acknowledging the significance of such previous pieces of work. These 'referentials' are much less frequently seen today – perhaps a reflection of the absence of a familiar literary and artistic background. The great cartoonist Vicky was famously told by his editor at *The New Chronicle* before the Second World War that he had to steep himself in British history, art and literature in order to be able to understand British life and draw effective cartoons about it. Vicky, the foreigner, used such images much more frequently than any other contemporary. In the present day Garland, who so much admired the work of Vicky, is the only major cartoonist to make frequent use of 'referentials'. John Jensen's cartoons based on Giacometti and Francis Bacon are on pages 32 and 85.

Cartoons based on previous cartoons provide an interesting sub-category of referentials. Some cartoons which had a particular impact in their time have been reproduced in their original form in articles and books to illustrate comments about events of that time. Later cartoonists have then drawn their own cartoons, referring to the original 'With acknowledgements to ....' So cartoonists make their modern representation based on Tenniel's 'Dropping the Pilot', or Low's 'Very well alone', or Zec's 'The Price of petrol has risen by one penny'.

The Impact of Cartoons

In order to take a view about the impact of cartoons, we have to consider the number of people who saw the cartoons. Cartoons impinged on the consciousness of a relatively small public originally through the sale and display of prints and later through collected folios of the works of, for example, Hogarth, Gillray and later H.B. *Punch*, published weekly, gave access probably to a wider range of the middle class, but the impact of cartoons was necessarily limited by the relatively small number of purchasers. As already mentioned, the impact of the wider provision of education, and technological changes in printing gave us more newspapers with large circulation. The caricaturists for *Vanity Fair*, *Ape* and *Spy*, (Leslie Ward)

provided for a relatively small circulation. Francis Carruthers Gould in *The Pall Mall Gazette* and *Westminster Gazette* was the first newspaper cartoonist to provide cartoons of significance on a wider basis.

As heavily promoted and widely circulated newspapers arrived, such as *The Daily Mail*, most popular papers had their own cartoonist – and in the circulation wars of the 1920s and 1930s the massive circulations of *The Daily Mail*, *The Daily Express*, *Sunday Express*, and *The Daily Herald* provided cartoons seen in each case by millions of readers. Low's significance arose not from the large circulation of *The Evening Standard*, but because of the importance of the particular group of readers centred on London. His rival on *The London Evening News* was Poy, and his other competition was Strube on *The Daily Express*. *The Daily Mail* had no cartoonist of similar impact to Strube, who also published an annual collection of his cartoons which showed the interest in his work.

Dyson, who had left *The Daily Herald* for the United States and Australia after the War, returned to *The Daily Herald* in 1931. Although these later cartoons are usually not thought to be as powerful as those he drew before 1920, he was still capable of making powerful attacks, particularly as an anti-Fascist.

The Daily Mirror in its various manifestations did not have a major cartoonist until Donald Zec during the Second World War. He was not as powerful or as interesting after the War. Vicky left the fading *News Chronicle* for *The Daily Mirror* at a time when it still had the largest circulation. *The Daily Mail* developed a major cartoonist – Illingworth – during the War. Although not himself seized with strong political beliefs, Illingworth's *Daily Mail* cartoons were certainly directly political even if based upon ideas given to him by others. Illingworth's successors on *The Daily Mail* included first Gerald Scarfe and Trog (Wally Fawkes). These equally powerful cartoonists were out of tune with the Mail's editorial line. Their successor was Mac, whose annual collection shows a generally gentler and often less strongly political line.

The *Daily Express* replaced Strube with

Cummings, a much more violent propagandist for Conservative views. Low briefly worked on *The Daily Herald* but was uncomfortable there in a straight Labour newspaper which was anyway declining from its position as a major circulation paper. There was a considerable gap on *The Evening Standard* after Low left in 1951 before Vicky joined; he attracted the same kind of criticism from an often conservative readership that Low had done.

If we exclude *The Morning Post*, later taken over by *The Daily Telegraph*, no Daily or Sunday heavy broadsheet newspapers had cartoons as a regular feature until Low moved to *The Guardian* in 1953. *The Telegraph* did not have a regular political cartoonist until 1966 and *The Times* until 1970. The Sunday heavies had cartoonists in *The Observer* from 1956, *The Sunday Times* from 1967, and *The Sunday Telegraph*, from its first issue in 1961.

The battle between the two original major heavyweight Sundays was for many years between Scarfe on *The Sunday Times* and Trog on *The Observer*. Scarfe's astonishing and grotesque exaggerations of figures were a surprising feature of *The Sunday Times*; Trog's critical views were conveyed in more traditionally mildly exaggerated physical representation, but often with a more stiletto form of wit. Jensen in *The Sunday Telegraph*, when it had arrived to compete with *The Sunday Times* and *The Observer*, gave an interestingly different view of the cartoonist's art, since he did not stick to a single style or technique.

Cummings provided cartoons for the Sunday version of *The Express* as well as the daily. But cartoons of the kind we are concerned with here were an irregular and declining feature of the major circulation *People* and *News of the World*, whose focus tended to be on issues of a personal and sexual mixture rather than general, social or political nature.

The political weeklies might be thought to be an obvious home for cartoons. Low's caricatures appeared as a supplement in *The New Statesman*, but cartoons did not appear as a regular feature until Vicky joined in 1954. *Tribune* and *Time and Tide* preceded *The New Statesman* by employing cartoonists, but they had even smaller circulations. *The Spectator*, the conservative rival, followed much later.

The cartoonists' life on a newspaper is often lengthy. When Les Gibbard took over from Papas in *The Guardian* he lasted for 25 years. Briefly he was published at the same time as Steve Bell, but the dramatic difference between their styles of cartooning was eventually resolved by Steve Bell becoming the major cartoonist – now partnered on Mondays by Martin Rowson. Garland has worked for *The Daily Telegraph* (with a five year sojourn at *The Independent*) since 1966. Peter Brookes has worked for *The Times* since 1982. Trog had 30 years on *The Observer* before he was replaced by Chris Riddell. Scarfe has been with *The Sunday Times* since 1967 whilst Cummings worked for 41 years on the *Daily* and *Sunday Express*.

This selective history of cartoonists in particular newspapers shows only that newspapers have generally been keen to provide cartoons. They must presumably think that they provide a significant addition to the strength of the paper. There is unfortunately very little other than anecdotal evidence to support this. This is not wholly surprising since there is very little substantial research on the influence of newspapers in general (the claim of *The Sun* about the 1992 election that it 'won it' for John Major has been decried even by its own political editor). Although editors have chosen to include political cartoonists, there are very few references to them in the editors' autobiographies. Scarfe, the most pungent of all cartoonists in the 1970s, is not referred to in Harold Evans' book about his period as editor of *The Sunday Times*.

Do cartoonists help to create a view or do they merely represent an already existing view? John Sergeant, then the BBC's Chief Political Correspondent, said that cartoons are able to capture in one space what journalists have spent days researching and ages talking about – and he might have added pages of newsprint writing about. It seems likely that they both represent existing views on some occasions and help to create it on others.

Cartoonists gave us the image of Nixon tangled up in tapes at the time of his discovered involvement in the Watergate break in. Cummings created images of Nye Bevan and Tony Benn which at least reinforced the many words written to assert that they were doctrinaire Left-wingers. The cartoonists' images of Margaret Thatcher portrayed her as alternatively an extremely strong woman or a savage destroyer of a supportive society. Images of Tony Blair originally as Bambi were less destructive of the public's perceptions of him than were the cartoons of Steve Bell portraying John Major as a wimp with his underpants outside his trousers. (Incidentally a complicated reference to Vicky's 'Supermac'.)

The large retrospective exhibition of Low's cartoons held in Westminster Hall in 2002 was accompanied by claims that Low was the 20th Century's greatest cartoonist. Michael Foot had commented earlier that Low's attacks on Hitler had met with considerable success. 'Low contributed more than any other single figure and as a result changed the atmosphere in the way people saw Hitler.' It is not clear whether Foot was actually talking about other cartoonists – otherwise those who remember Winston Churchill's contributions before 1939 would be strongly inclined to disagree. Foot had also argued that Low's cartoon of the double-headed coalition ass helped to destroy Lloyd George's coalition in 1922. At other times Foot has identified Vicky as the supreme cartoonist, so we can be sure that Foot at least amongst ex-editors rated cartoonists highly. We do know that Hitler was gravely displeased by Low's cartoons, attempted to have them banned from *The Evening Standard*, and ensured that Low was placed on the death list of people who would be killed when Germany took over Britain.

The effect on the 'victims'

Lear's question 'who can tell me who I am' is answered by some cartoons, as it is recognised by some victims. The earliest case of a politician affected by cartoons is that of Tweed, the American politician who said that his constituents would not read comments about him but that he was annoyed by 'them dammed pictures'. Stanley Baldwin was upset although he did not threaten such disastrous consequences as did Hitler. In 1935 he expressed his preference for Sidney Strube of *The Daily Express*, 'Strube is a gentle genius … I don't mind his attacks because he never hits below the belt. Now Low is a genius but he is evil and malicious. I cannot bear Low!' Vicky certainly upset the readers of *The Evening Standard* from time to time. A Lieutenant Colonel G.M. Thompson said of a Vicky cartoon that it was 'a masterpiece of Socialist propaganda, vulgar, vindictive and misleading'. The later and generally much less political *Evening Standard* cartoonist, Jak, produced at least two cartoons which threatened the production of *The Evening Standard*, about electricians and about Irish people (which led to the withdrawal of the Greater London Council advertising). Cartoons have been referred to the Press Council and its predecessors, but no cartoonist has yet been fined or taken off to jail. The threat to *The Guardian* and its cartoonist Steve Bell from the Scottish industrialist, Brian Souter, showed that he felt deeply insulted, but in the end he withdrew his proposed civil case against them.

One particularly interesting question is whether cartoons influence Lords. In the first place, this depends on whether they see cartoons, and this most often will relate to the newspapers they choose to read. *The Times* ran an advertising campaign 'Top People Read the *Times*' but this may not have been based on detailed research of Lords as a group. The image of gloved servants ironing a copy of *The Times* before handing it to his Lordship is unlikely to be accurate today.

It is interesting to see which autobiographies include cartoons, which may indicate an awareness of them. Baroness Thatcher includes none – Lords Home and Heseltine do. Generally autobiographies and most biographies do not include strongly critical cartoons.

Perceptions of Lords other than in relation to particular individuals have been easily perhaps somewhat facilely based on drawing them in their ermine and coronets for almost any occasion on which Lords are displayed. The fact that, of course, these historic

CARTOONS AND CARICATURE IN THE UNITED KINGDOM

costumes are not worn for the general activities of the House of Lords but only for special occasions such as the State Opening of Parliament does not prevent cartoonists from using them as a way of showing that Lords are very different.

Cartoonists about themselves

David Low wrote more about the purposes and art of cartooning than any other cartoonist. His style of cartooning, particularly in comparison with modern successors on *The Guardian* represents his strong views about the best way in which to present his ideas. He wrote that 'no artist in caricature purely can do good work on malice. It clouds the judgement. The immoderate exaggeration inspired by malice is apt to become as tedious as too much slapstick in a farce ... brutality almost invariably defeats itself.' During the Second World War Low said, at a time of particular temptation to draw differently, 'the horrific cartoon is not an effective political approach in this war. What the dictator does not want to get around is the idea that he is an ass, which is really damaging.'

Ralph Steadman's work which is usually savage with faces and bodies that are grotesque said 'obviously something troubles me about the world or I wouldn't be so bitter. It has got at me in a way I can't quite understand. It knows something I don't know, therefore I resent it and hit out in as violent a way as I can in my drawings. You can say things in a drawing that you cannot say in words.' He also said, 'If (a cartoon) does not feel uncomfortable, ridicule and provide insight on an intellectual level, what is the cartoon's purpose? If it is not a corrective of some sort, it plays the politician's game and wallows in the realm of light entertainment. It must be said that the cartoon's purpose is not just to be funny. It is a sad fact but oppression, deceit and injustice are the mothers of satire – the cartoonist's best weapon.' Steadman has stopped drawing politicians because he believes their egos are stroked by cartoons.

Gerald Scarfe has pessimistic views about the impact of his cartoons. 'Looking back on this record (in 1982), I have no feeling that any cartoon has ever changed the course of events.' 'My drawings are often a cry against that which I detest, and in showing my dislike I have to draw the dislikeable.'

Cummings' view was that 'the cartoon can deliver its message in a flash, whereas a leading article needs ten minute's reading to get its political message delivered.' He also said about a cartoonist that 'he disposes of an element of power. He can by constant repetition create an image of a politician to a large section of the voting public'.

Steve Bell's view of his work is nicely illustrated by his comment: 'It took me several years before I realised that Margaret Thatcher was a psychopath. Conversely, it took less than a month to see that John Major was a mega-nerd.'

George Townshend remains unique as a peer who published cartoons. Even after the opportunity presented by the Life Peerages Act of 1959, no cartoonist has been elevated to the peerage. A number however have been knighted: Tenniel, Francis Carruthers Gould, Leslie Ward (Spy), Max Beerbohm and Bernard Partridge. The last, perhaps particularly appropriately, was David Low. If we look at present day cartoonists, it seems unlikely in the case of some of them that they would be offered a knighthood – and equally unlikely in most cases that they would accept it.

3

Personalities of 18th and 19th Centuries

The Peers most frequently shown in cartoons and caricatures during this period were primarily politicians. The most prominent amongst these of course were prime ministers – there were twenty three 'Lordly' prime ministers in these two centuries. It was the norm for prime ministers to have a title, though they did not all sit in the House of Lords. However Lord Kenneth Baker's book *The Prime Ministers* has covered the field in full detail, and only four are illustrated in this chapter. Additional cartoons for this period are shown in the chapters on the Army and Navy, Sporting Peers and Ladies. The relatively small number of cartoons nonetheless indicates some of the changes in style and content – from the scatological cartoon by Townshend to the wholly decorous portrayal by Tenniel of Disraeli and Queen Victoria. The first cartoon by Hogarth is interesting not only because of the person it depicts, but because Hogarth here moved

Simon Fraser, 12th Lord Lovat, 1667–1747

Caricature by Hogarth of the last peer to be beheaded for treason. Hogarth's unexaggerated drawing nonetheless brings out, through his narrow eyes and slight smile, an essentially unattractive character.

Profile

Fraser acquired the succession to the Barony by violent means, and followed with treachery to William III. He was arrested, pardoned, exiled to France, returned from France, maintained his association with first the Old Pretender (the exiled son of James II) and finally the Young Pretender (grandson of James II). He attempted to 'raise the clans' in Scotland in aid of the Jacobite Rebellion, was eventually captured and beheaded for treason.

away from his more familiar general studies – his *Election* series and the *Rakes Progress*. Hogarth always wanted to be remembered as an artist rather than as a social or political commentator, but he was not successful in this. Gillray became the leader, following earlier but much less effective work, in the field of significant physical exaggeration. The cartoons by Tenniel and 'Ape' are characteristic of the Victorian period of cartooning which was almost entirely bland.

The Scotch Broomstick and the Female Besom

The Earl of Bute's encounter with George III's mother.

Profile

George II had thought the 3rd Earl of Bute to be the very man to be envoy at some small provincial German court where there is nothing to do. Bute (1713–1792) made a nonsense of this proposition by being made Principal Secretary of State, in effect Prime Minister, in 1762. His capacity for intrigue included the association believed to exist between himself and George III's mother, as shown in the suggestive cartoon by George Townshend in 1762. Bute was otherwise often drawn in cartoons as a Boot – a verbal pun which appears in a rather different form later with Wellington.

A SPENCER & a THREADPAPER.

Pub.^d May 17.th 1792 by H. Humphrey N.º 18 Old Bond Street

A Spencer and a Thread Paper

In this, the most exaggerated of the three Gillray cartoons in this chapter, the 2nd Earl of Spencer (1758–1834) is shown in a new style of overcoat. This double-breasted overcoat without tails in fact became known as a 'Spencer'. The slender figure next to him has not been identified. A thread paper was a folded paper which contained threads, but also described a person of very slender figure.

The 5th Duke of Marlborough 1766–1840

Again this is one of Gillray's less exaggerated caricatures.

Profile

In her biography of him, Mary Soames describes him as the 'Profligate Duke'. The cartoon was published in 1803, before he inherited the Dukedom in 1817. He was immensely keen on gardens and plants and spent what even then were huge sums of money on creating gardens, and building the Great Lake at Blenheim Palace. He became bankrupt except for those aspects of his inheritance which were entailed. He was the subject of a major scandal when he was accused of 'criminal conversation' (adultery) with his best friend's wife, through whom he had a daughter. Subsequently he had three more daughters through another mistress.

Earl of Shaftesbury (1801–1885)

This cartoon was published in Vanity Fair in 1869 by Ape (Carlo Pellegrini).

Profile

Shaftesbury was an MP from 1826–1851 when he inherited the Earldom. He was the first legislator to be associated with primary reform of social conditions. This included reform of the lunacy laws, protection for factory and mine workers and chimney sweeps, and generally better housing for the poor. He said that 'I cannot bear to leave the world with all the misery in it.' His social views were closely associated with his Christian evangelism, which sometimes led to mockery. His strength of view, inevitably seen by some critics as arrogance, is well conveyed in the cartoon.

SUSANNAH AND THE ELDERS

Susannah and the Elders

This cartoon in 1837 by HB (John Doyle) shows the young Queen Victoria with two senior advisers Palmerston (left) and Melbourne.

Profile

Lord Melbourne (1779–1848) was an MP before inheriting the title in 1829. He was Prime Minister twice, the last time for six years. He is particularly well known as adviser to the young Queen Victoria until he retired in 1841. He gave perhaps one of the earliest indications of the rule that cabinet members were all supposed to speak with one voice. At the end of discussion in cabinet about the Corn Laws, he is supposed to have said 'Now is it to lower the price of corn or isn't it? It is not much matter which we say, but mind, we must all say the same.' Not necessarily in connection with this, he also said 'What I want is men who will support me when I am in the wrong.' The generally pragmatic line of British political life is supported by his comment that 'Nobody ever did anything very foolish except from strong principles.'

Profile

Palmerston (1784–1865) became Prime Minister in 1855, and served in that role for a total of eight years. He had previously been Foreign Secretary for eleven years, which was the role he had at the time of this cartoon. The bland supportive role shown in this cartoon relates neither to his aggressive conduct of foreign affairs, nor to his conduct of a different sort of affair. He was said to have had relations with one of Queen Victoria's Ladies of Waiting, amongst others. Both he and Melbourne were cited in divorce actions. Their merits as political mentors of the young Queen Victoria are sharply in contrast with a relatively obvious sexual activity out of tune with much of the Victorian age.

Empress Earl

This cartoon shows the Queen making Disraeli Earl of Beaconsfield in 1876, and refers to the fact that he had earlier caused her to be created Empress of India. Tenniel's cartoon of that event showed a much more Jewish looking Disraeli.

Profile

The Earl of Beaconsfield (1804–1881), Benjamin Disraeli, has claims to be the most astonishing political figure of the 19th Century. The arrival of Ted Heath and later Margaret Thatcher as Leader of the Conservative Party in the 20th Century scarcely bears comparison with the rise of Disraeli, from a family of Jewish origin. Not only did he become an exciting orator with a gift for vituperation, but he dressed in a way which would cause people to identify him easily. Shouted down in his first speech in the Commons he famously said 'The time will come when you will hear me.' He wrote novels many of them with political themes which related to his own convictions. In his novel *Sybil* he described 'Two nations, between whom there is no intercourse and no sympathy; who are as ignorant of each other's habits, thoughts and feelings as if they were dwellers in different zones.' This idea is sustained in some of the arguments in today's Conservative Party. Unlike his great contemporary Gladstone he developed an ease of relationship with Queen Victoria which saved him a lot of trouble: he commented 'Everyone likes flattery; and when you come to royalty you should lay it on with a trowel.' When he became Prime Minister he said 'I have climbed to the top of the greasy pole.'

SANDWICH-CARROTS! dainty SANDWICH-CARROTS

John Montagu, 5th Earl of Sandwich 1743–1814

As with the Townshend cartoon relating to Bute, the sexual innuendo is clear – one commentator describes Sandwich as showing 'brazen lechery'.

Profile

The 4th Earl of Sandwich gave his name both to the Sandwich Islands and perhaps apocryphally to the food creation. The 5th Earl however had no equivalent distinction – the cartoon is a personal attack on a politically unimportant figure. This is one of Gillray's less exaggerated drawings, showing what can be done by suggestion rather than by explicit outrage as in some of his other cartoons.

The People's Budget and Lords Reform

4

After the passage of the Reform Act of 1832, the primacy of the Commons over the Lords had been more finally established – their relationship followed a convention that, although the Lords could and did reject Bills of other kinds (see especially Home Rule) they did not reject Money Bills. In 1909 the Chancellor of the Exchequer David Lloyd George proposed tax increases, including Death Duties which the Lords saw as being explicitly directed at themselves. In one sense they were undoubtedly right since Lloyd George claimed that the Lords and explicitly the Dukes of Westminster and Northumberland represented a class which did nothing to justify its retention and passing on of great wealth. He talked about unearned increment. This led to one of his characteristic witticisms. When asked for his definition of this term by William Joynson-Hicks who had recently added the name of his rich wife to his own, he replied 'The best example of the unearned increment is the hyphen in the Hon member's name.'

A prolonged battle then ensued in the House of Lords. Lansdowne and Halsbury led the revolt, the plurality against the Liberal Budget being substantially enhanced by Peers who had never or scarcely ever attended – 'backwoods men'.

However two general elections in January and December 1910 produced a continuation of the Liberal Government now propped up by eighty Irish Nationalists. King George V had promised Asquith, the Prime Minister, that he would if necessary ennoble enough people in order to secure passage of the Budget. Lansdowne eventually led the climb down in the Lords which enabled passage of the Budget, and subsequently the passing of the Bill which became the Parliament Act of 1912. (The two sides of the argument in Conservative ranks had been called Hedgers and Ditchers i.e. last Ditches). Like the proverbial Duke of York, Lansdowne had marched his Peers up to the top of the hill and then back down again.

This huge constitutional impasse caused the complaints about the power of hereditary peers to be turned into an Act which substantially reduced those powers. As we were frequently reminded during the later debates on reform of the House of Lords, the preamble to the Act had said that all hereditaries would be excluded 'within the term of the present government'. In fact no change in the composition of the Lords was proposed in the Act, the most significant part of which was to give the Lords the power to delay anything other than a Money Bill but only for two years.

An Heroic Resolve

In this cartoon Asquith is opposed by the ex Prime Minister and still then Leader of the Conservative Party, Arthur James Balfour (1848–1930). 'Dukes' is a pun on a slang word for fists.

AN HEROIC RESOLVE.

MASTER HERBERT: "Look here, Arthur. I'll never fight you again, if you're allowed to "put up your dukes". So there!'

Profile

Herbert Henry Asquith (1852–1928), was a strong supporter of Lloyd George on the Budget issue (and later on reforming the House of Lords). Of middle class origin, he was the first British Prime Minister to achieve that position without the support of significant landed estates. As Chancellor of the Exchequer from 1906 under Campbell Bannerman he introduced differential tax rates for earned and unearned incomes and non-contributory old age pensions. As Prime Minister from 1908–1916 he presided over the major innovations in state financed Welfare, and then led us into war with Germany in 1914. He was replaced as Prime Minister by Lloyd George in December 1916. This led to a split in the Liberal Party and to an accelerating decline in its fortunes. He was created Earl of Oxford and Asquith in 1925.

Particularly because of his perceived lack of strong leadership in the First World War, he became associated posthumously with an earlier comment related to what he would do about the House of Lords 'We had better wait and see'. In fact he led a very talented Government with great effect up to 1914. He was a powerful orator who managed to remain both erect and coherent despite a considerable intake of alcohol. Bonar Law, who replaced Balfour said of him 'Asquith when drunk can make a better speech than any of us sober'.

"KICKING THE BUCKET."

ASQUITH : "You won't dare kick it away with that rope round your neck!"
HIS LORDSHIP : "Won't I? You don't know what I may have behind me!"

Profile

The view of Arthur James, Earl Balfour (1848–1930) as a lethargic figure was expressed by contemporaries and seized on by cartoonists. (See Chapter 5). The accuracy of this view might be supported by his own belief that 'Nothing matters very much and very few things matter at all.' However he was certainly active enough to acquire the title 'Bloody Balfour' when he was Chief Secretary in Ireland in the 1880s. Nor was his succession to the Prime Ministership to his Uncle the Marquess of Salisbury in 1902 seen at the time as simply nepotic. His government went down to a massive defeat by the Liberals in the Election of January 1906. He continued to have an uncomfortable time as Leader of the Party, but survived a Balfour Must Go campaign until he resigned in 1911 when the die-hards in the House of Lords refused to accept his advice.

His political career continued when he joined the war time coalition government in 1915. He became Foreign Secretary in 1916 in Lloyd George's coalition. His ambition and perseverance were registered by the fact that having departed from office with Lloyd George in 1922, he returned under Baldwin in 1925.

It was Balfour who wrote on behalf of the Government in 1917 'His Majesty's Government views with favour the establishment in Palestine of a national home for the Jewish people and will use its best endeavours to facilitate this object.' The second half of this statement is less frequently quoted 'It being clearly understood that nothing shall be done which may prejudice the civil and religious rights of existing non-Jewish communities in Palestine.'

Profile

Henry the Fifth Marquess of Lansdowne (1845–1927) had been Governor General of Canada, Viceroy of India, War Minister and finally Foreign Secretary (1900–1906). He was the Leader of the Conservatives in the House of Lords when the dispute first over the 1909 Budget and then over the Parliament Bill was fought out. He joined the first war time coalition administration under Asquith and circulated a memorandum on the possibility of peace which was disowned by his colleagues.

It is interesting to compare the view of public opinion expressed in this cartoon with that 'Temptation and Retribution' in the cartoon shown later.

Putting a Good Face on it

Partridge shows Lansdowne late in the day trying his own version of Lords Reform; this was rejected by the Liberal Government.

PUTTING A GOOD FACE ON IT

LORD LANSDOWNE: ' Say this house is badly conducted, do they? And mean to stop the licence? Ah, but they haven't seen my coat of whitewash yet. That ought to make 'em think twice.'

WILL HE LET IT PASS ?

LORD LANSDOWNE (waiting for the Budget): I wish I could chop its head off without killing it altogether.
But he can't.

Bills presented in either the Commons or the Lords were, in a Victorian cartoonist's cliché, always presented in this form, as a continuous round document. Lansdowne is dressed conventionally from the cartoonist's point of view in his top half, but the doublet and hose has no apparent connection or significance.

Temptation and Retribution

Leo Cheney's cartoon is of interest because it gives a quite different view of public opinion than that shown in Kicking the Bucket.

TEMPTATION

RETRIBUTION

Who Said Reform?

In this cartoon by FCG, Halsbury appears here as a dog emerging from a kennel formed by a Lordly Coronet.

Profile

The Earl of Halsbury was Lord Chancellor for a total of seventeen years, twice under Salisbury and then under Balfour. He accepted in the Parliament of 1906–1910 the relatively moderate opposition offered to Liberal measures in the House of Lords under the Tory Leader, Lord Lansdowne. However when it came to the Parliament Act of 1911 at the age of eighty eight he formed and led a group of Peers known as the Die-hards. They went to the wire in opposing the Bill, which only passed by the narrow majority of seventeen.

THE OLD TROJAN

LORD LANSDOWNE: 'Don't lug that infernal machine into the citadel. The thing's full of enemies.'
LORD HALSBURY: "I know. That's where my heroism comes in.'

The Old Trojan

This cartoon by Bernard Partridge suggests that Halsbury and Lansdowne were actually acting together in an attempt to avoid the creation of five hundred Liberal Peers – but in fact they were separated in the final vote. The figure of 500 was that thought necessary to ensure a majority for the Government – but Lloyd George had earlier commented about the House of Lords 'A body of five hundred men chosen at random amongst the unemployed'. Of course the reference to the Trojan Horse would have been very familiar to people at that time, much more educated in classical myth and history than people would be today.

The D....D Consequences

Lansdowne here as the sub-title shows is indicating his reluctant acceptance of a death blow to the Lords.

THE NEW GUY FAWKES PLOT
OR, THE BEST ADVERTISED CONSPIRACY IN THE WORLD
[The First Autumn Meeting of the Cabinet has been summoned for the Fifth of November, Guy Fawkes Day.]

The New Guy Fawkes Plot

This cartoon by Linley Sambourne shows that even in 1907 the House of Lords was an issue with potentially explosive contents. Although the cartoon seems to show Lloyd George as the energising figure, the leader in front is Prime Minister Henry Campbell-Bannerman.

Profile

Henry Campbell-Bannerman (1836–1908) served in governments under Gladstone and Rosebery. Without ambition originally to be Leader, he finished up as such because of the continuing factions within the Liberal Party. He acquired national fame by his opposition to what he called 'Methods of Barbarism' in the War against the Boers. An attempt to push him upstairs to the House of Lords before he became Prime Minister in 1906, in effect a conspiracy led by Gray, Haldane and Asquith failed as he showed determination in avoiding this fate. He then pushed through the early Liberal Government measures such as the Trades Disputes Bill. He is unique in the 20th Century in that he actually died while Prime Minister.

The Chance of a Lifetime

This cartoon by L Raven-Hill shows that the opportunities involved in creating five hundred Peers were well recognised by Asquith and Lloyd George. The trade in Peerages, although not to the extent of five hundred, was by now well established. (See later chapter on 'Scandals' for further discussion of this).

Profile

In David Lloyd George's (1863–1945) early life he was a whole-hearted radical in relation to the ownership of land. A leader amongst the minority who opposed the Boer War, then through his 1909 Budget a radical on social provision and taxes to pay for welfare benefits, Lloyd George became 'The man

THE CHANCE OF A LIFETIME.

Our Mr. Asquith. "FIVE HUNDRED CORONETS, DIRT-CHEAP! THIS LINE OF GOODS OUGHT TO MAKE BUSINESS A BIT BRISKER, WHAT?"
Our Mr. Lloyd George. "NOT HALF; BOUND TO GO LIKE HOT CAKES."

who won the war' as Prime Minister of the Coalition set up in 1916. He won the 'Coupon Election' with Conservatives and his Liberal supporters in 1918. This formalised his split from Asquith and Liberals. The Conservatives who formed a majority in his support decided to bring down the Coalition in 1922. Stanley Baldwin a senior but not the leading Conservative said of Lloyd George 'a dynamic force is a very terrible thing; it may crush you but it is not necessarily right.'

Although the Liberals were eventually formally reunited, they were replaced by Labour as the main opposition to the Conservative Party, and Lloyd George was never close to having power himself again. He was seen by his opponents as an unprincipled opportunist, and by those who were seduced by his great personal charm as the radical pre war reformer and successful war leader. Maynard Keynes described him as 'This goat footed bard'. This referred to his skill in moving from one position to another as he 'got things done'. In the minds of other people, the goat referred to his sexual adventures. The fact that these were largely concealed from the public is astonishing in the 21st Century. After earlier adventures, he largely settled down with Frances Stevenson as his permanent mistress. More relevant scandals might have brought him down – the Marconi affair and the Lloyd George fund (see Chapter 17). However the real memorial to him is not in these aspects of his life but in his contribution to winning the war and to improving the lives of poorer people, and his redesign of cabinet government. When they went to the post office to draw their benefit, tears of gratitude would run down the cheek of some, and they would say as they picked up their money, 'God bless that Lloyd George'! (F Thompson in Larkrise to Candelford).

The wit with which he supported his extraordinary eloquence was shown on his response to the claim that the House of Lords was 'the watchdog of the constitution'. 'It is Mr Balfour's Poodle' (1908). With the exception of Will Dyson, cartoonists such as Low, Strube and Poy tended to show Lloyd George as a twinkling imp rather than as a dynamic force.

5

Political Personalities of 20th and 21st Centuries

Whereas the previous chapter, though mainly centred on political personalities, included two non-political figures, this chapter is purely political. Later chapters give the opportunity to look at non-political figures of this time.

The volume of cartoon and caricature had expanded hugely in this period. There are simply more cartoons and many more people available. If all the good cartoons of significant political personalities were to be included, we would need a separate volume, even if only one cartoon per personality was the allowance.

Given the need for selectivity, what kind of criteria were used? Should all Prime Ministers who became Peers be included, simply because of the distinction of their position? Which other major political leaders ought to be included – for example which leaders of opposition parties, which cabinet ministers? In the end it came down to a personal judgement on the quality and effectiveness of the cartoon, the potential interest in the individual or situation being illustrated. Even these broad criteria do not explain all the cartoons; some are included simply because the compiler for this book liked them.

No general historical survey is included here; the political context is provided with each cartoon.

Lord Birkenhead (1872–1930)

Profile

David Low in other cartoons portrayed Birkenhead as 'bursting head', a reference to both his arrogant intellect and his alcoholic consumption. He was not alone in his liking for alcohol. He famously advised the Labour minister who complained of 'an ell of an eadache' to 'take a couple of aspirates'. His maiden speech in January 1906 set the standard for all subsequent

'maidens', in defying the usual rule of not being controversial. Violently opposed to Home Rule in Ireland before the war, when he was called 'galloper Smith', he helped negotiate the eventual treaty in 1921. He served as Attorney General in November 1915, as Lord Chancellor in January 1919 but left the Government with Lloyd George in 1922. He returned as Secretary of State for India in 1924. In his address as Rector of Glasgow University in 1923 he said that 'The world continues to offer glittering prizes to those who have stout hearts and sharp swords' often an eloquent expression of at least one part of Conservative philosophy.

A Tale of Two Houses

Sub-titled – It is a far far stranger thing I do than – a reference to Dickens' *Tale of Two Cities*. The transformation from the son of a skilled artisan in a small Welsh village was complete. David Lloyd George became Earl Lloyd George of Dwyfor in January 1945. As E H Shepard's cartoon and its subtitle show, his decision to take his peerage was in contrast with his earlier attitude to the Lords.

George Curzon, Marquess of Kedleston (1859–1925)

Harry Furniss captures the rigidity and hauteur of Curzon's manner in public. He was described as a 'very superior person'.

Profile

Appointed Viceroy of India at the age of 39 he commenced his upward mobility through Baron, Viscount, Earldom and finally Marquess in 1921. He acquired the means to support himself in grand style by marrying, probably for love, the American heiress Mary Leiter. He served in the War Cabinet under Lloyd George and became Foreign Secretary in 1919. His relationship with Lloyd George was difficult and he was one of the major Conservatives who helped to bring him down at the Carlton Club. Foreign Secretary under Bonar Law he developed the expectation that he would succeed Law as Prime Minister. King George V chose Baldwin partly because he was persuaded of Curzon's unpopularity amongst colleagues and the general public, partly by reference to the unsuitability of a Prime of Minister in the House of Lords. His view that 'The best work in the world was always done by members of the aristocracy' was clearly not accepted in his own case. Baldwin reported that when he met Curzon subsequently 'I got the sort of greeting a corpse would have given an undertaker.' In the 1920s Curzon was out of touch with the times. During the war he had said on seeing some soldiers bathing 'I did not know the lower orders had such white skins'.

Earl of Balfour

This cartoon by Bert Thomas conveys the languid air mentioned in the profile in the previous chapter.

Wedgwood Benn

Lord Stansgate (1877–1960)

Low conveys his physical stature cleverly. He was a small man who was explosive in debate. Churchill said of him 'The Hon Member must really not develop more indignation than he can contain.'

Profile

William Wedgwood Benn, Lord Stansgate, resigned as a Liberal MP to join the Labour Party and served in the Commons for all but five years in the period 1927–1940. He was Secretary of State for India from 1929–1931, and Secretary of State for Air 1945–1946. It was his elevation to the Peerage in 1940 which vicariously brought about a major change in the constitution, and justifies his inclusion here. When he died in 1960 his son Anthony Neil Wedgwood Benn precipitated, as described in Chapter 15, the process by which individuals who inherited a peerage could disclaim it.

There is Nothing Like Adventure

Vicky in 1944 comments satirically on the opponents of Beveridge's social security proposals.

Profile

William Beveridge later Baron Beveridge of Tuggal (1879–1963) was a civil servant and academic whose main fame is that of a social reformer, especially with the production of the Beveridge Report in 1942. In the Civil Service he was personal assistant to Winston Churchill when he was President of the Board of Trade, and had later more senior positions in the Civil Service. From 1919–1937 he was the Director of the London School of Economics. He returned to the Civil Service and worked on the report on Social Insurance and Allied Services which acquired his name and which generated huge public interest. 'Want is one only of five giants on the road on reconstruction... the others are Disease, Ignorance, Squalor and Idleness.' The Report advocated a free National Health Service, family allowances, Government maintained full employment and a universal subsistence level of social insurance – the basis of the Welfare State the Labour Government of 1945 later set in train.

Earl Attlee

This cartoon by Cummings attempts apparently to show a difference between the essential Attlee in workman's trousers and boots and Attlee as Earl. Although a nice cartoonist's fantasy, it has no relation to Attlee's actual life (1883–1967) as a largely conventional middle class leader of the Labour Party.

Profile

Attlee's first break with convention was brought about by experience in working with poor people in the East End of London. A major in the First World War, and then an MP he was a minor figure in the Labour Government of 1929–1931. His survival in the Labour cataclysm of 1931 led to his becoming leader of the Labour Party in 1935. Hugh Dalton one of his major contemporaries said of him 'and a mouse shall lead them.' He was a very successful Deputy to Churchill during the Second World War; other members of the Cabinet particularly appreciated his ability to get the business done, rather than having to listen to Churchill most of the time (Attlee later tartly commented to Churchill 'A monologue is not a dialogue'.). There are different views about his achievements as Labour Prime Minister largely depending on whether you believe the Labour Government was a 'good thing', particularly in the tough economic circumstances after 1945. His ability to manage the many extraordinary personalities in his Cabinet such as Bevin, Bevan and Cripps suggest he had capacity not tested in Tony Blair. He was not an exhilarating public speaker, and in the conduct of business tended to favour the view that he would not use one word where none would do. Churchill is supposed to have said of him that he was a 'modest little man, with plenty to be modest about'. Attlee wrote his own retaliation in the form of a poem:

> 'Few thought he was even a starter
> There were many who thought
>   themselves smarter
> But he ended PM CH and OM
> An Earl and a Knight of the Garter.'

Lord Home 'A solid chap'

John Jensen's cartoon shows how little physically Alec Douglas Home resembled this description – and of course exaggerated his facial features.

Profile

Like Attlee and John Major, Home (1903–1995) was a cricket enthusiast. As Lord Dunglass, he was a Conservative MP and indeed appeared literally carrying the bag for Neville Chamberlain on the latter's return from the Munich conversation with Hitler in 1938. From 1951 he progressed up the ministerial ladder as Scottish Secretary, Commonwealth Relations Secretary and finally Foreign Secretary. When Macmillan resigned as Prime Minister in October 1963, Home backed into the limelight and became Prime Minister, never previously having figured amongst the likely successors. He took advantage, as his rival Hailsham had done, of the opportunity to disclaim his peerage. He held on as Prime Minister for a year before being beaten by Harold Wilson in the Election of 1964. Although he

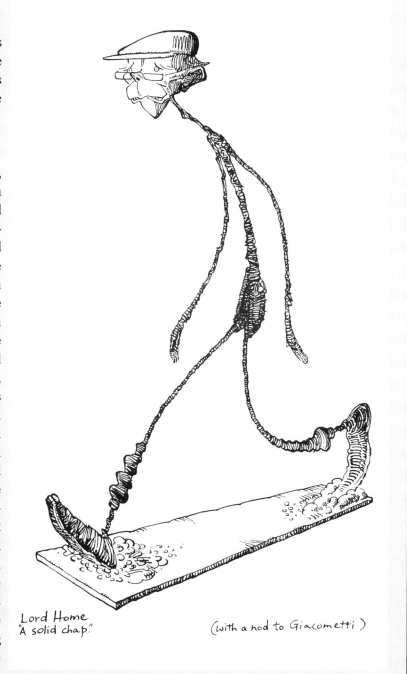

Lord Home
'A solid chap.'

(with a nod to Giacometti)

tartly replied to Wilson's description of him as the 14th Earl by saying that Mr Wilson was no doubt the 14th Mr Wilson, he was otherwise unsuccessful in competing with Wilson. He made a mistake in confessing in public that when he was considering economic documents he would take out a box of matches and start moving them around. In many ways he carried the British art of self-deprecation too far. In his autobiography he reported disarmingly that one make up artist abandoned her attempt to make him look any better, because she said he had a head like a skull. Cartoonists' emphasis on his face seemed very savage at the time – although now we see representations of major politicians which manage to produce grotesqueries from quite normal faces. Home is better remembered for his sense of public duty, and his loyalty to Edward Heath (a relationship which neither Margaret Thatcher nor Edward Heath thought it necessary to emulate). He accepted a life peerage as Lord Home of the Hirsel in 1974.

Lord Jenkins of Hillhead (1920–2003)

As the cartoon indicates, Jenkins increasingly relished the good things in life. His supposed addiction to claret became a cartoonist's cliché with which he became bored. British political life is replete with politicians who might have become Prime Minister. Roy Jenkins reached the level at which this became a serious proposition. The son of a Welsh National Union of Mineworkers official, who served a term in prison for inciting a strike, he disposed of all physical and political connections with that kind of life. After war service he became a Labour MP and wrote a rather thin biography of Attlee which started him on a literary path. A devotee of Hugh Gaitskell, and shattered by his death, he

expected little when Wilson formed his Government in 1964. Wilson however appointed him as Minister for Aviation, and he then achieved what many regarded as his high peak as Home Secretary. Although subsequently castigated by his opponents for having encouraged the 'permissive' society, he referred to it as the 'civilised' society. The line he took on homosexuality, abortion and the abolition of flogging in prisons has never been reversed. Wilson appointed him in 1967 as Chancellor of the Exchequer, in which role he is often given the accolade of being 'one of the best' since 1945. In 1971 however as Deputy Leader he effectively ruined his chances of becoming Labour Prime Minister by voting against his party on entering into the European Economic Community. He opposed setting up the referendum on retaining our membership, but then proceeded to help win it. He was beaten by Jim Callaghan in the election to provide a successor to Wilson in 1976, and became instead the first British President of the EEC. His disenchantment with the Labour Party led eventually to attempting to 'break the mould' of British politics through the formation of the Social Democratic Party in 1981. The SDP did not break the mould – but arguably led to the eventual creation of New Labour. His first major literary effort started relevantly for this book with *Mr Balfour's Poodle*, and concluded with huge biographies of Gladstone and Churchill which were immensely successful. Readers of this book who will remember him in his later years as a plummy voiced speaker unable to articulate his 'R's may not realise that he was one of the most effective debaters of his political generation.

'I Suppose You've Had A Busy Day At The Office'

This Trog cartoon in 1971 refers to Longford's investigation into various aspects of the sex industry. Whether his wife Elizabeth was quite so insouciant is not known.

Profile

The 7th Earl of Longford (1905–2001), whose untitled name was Frank Pakenham was a Junior Minister under Attlee, and then a Cabinet Minister under Wilson; he resigned from the Government in 1968 in protest at the postponement of the school leaving age to 16. He would merit attention as one of the very few ministers to resign over a matter of policy. His deep Christian beliefs had made him seem rather unworldly often as a minister. His general and particular attention to penal reform kept him in the public eye; he sometimes gave the impression of being more concerned to help the sinner than to pay attention to those sinned against. He certainly did not choose the easy path when dealing with criminals, such as Myra Hindley.

His visits to, for example, Denmark in pursuit of research on pornography were easy targets for cartoonists. His deep sincerity was not always accompanied by good judgement, nor was he lacking in ego. This latter point added to the number of jokes about him, such as his supposed complaint to a bookshop that they were not displaying his book *Humility* in the window.

We Shall Defend What's Left Of Our Islands

In this cartoon 5 April 1982 Lord Carrington is displayed defending the Falkland Islands. At this date he was Foreign Secretary in Margaret Thatcher's Government.

Profile

Lord Carrington (1919–) had worked his way up the ministerial ladder under Prime Ministers from Churchill onwards. His diplomatic triumphs in the Foreign Office included some effective negotiations in Europe for which he was not thanked by Margaret Thatcher, and the negotiation of a settlement in free elections in what became Zimbabwe.

He is included in this book because he resigned shortly after this cartoon in 1982 as he took responsibility, more than many believed appropriate, for the failure of British policy and action over the Falkland Islands. The last hereditary peer to hold such high office, he was also the last cabinet minister to resign on such principled grounds.

Lord Arnold Goodman

This caricature by Marc highlights relatively delicately the extent to which Goodman was overweight, and also manages to indicate the main theme of his life, which was to influence other people.

Profile

Lord Goodman (1913–1995) acted at a political level as an adviser to Harold Wilson and also to Edward Heath. He managed to combine a very successful career as a lawyer while carrying on negotiations at a political level as one of the many people who attempted to secure a negotiated settlement with Smith of Rhodesia. His incredibly busy days were not complicated by any attachments in his domestic life. His public roles included Chairmanship of the Arts Council, Mastership of an Oxford College, Chair of the *Observer* Newspaper and prime involvement in the founding of the National Theatre.

'In Fact You've Never Had it so Bad'

The cartoon reference (20th January 1985) is to Macmillan's claim in 1957 that people had 'never had it so good'.

Profile

We have seen Harold Macmillan, Earl of Stockton (1894–1986), in the introduction by John Jensen. He delayed taking his traditional peerage until 1984 long after his resignation in 1963. In 1985 he was antipathetic to the economic policies of Margaret Thatcher.

As Chancellor of the Exchequer he managed both to encourage Eden to go into his Suez campaign in 1956, and to come out when it was in progress thus acquiring the jibe from Harold Wilson that he was 'First in, first out'. The 'usual consultations' led to him being elected Leader of the Tory Party rather than R A Butler when Eden resigned in 1957. Part of his subsequent opposition to Margaret Thatcher was due to the fact that if faced with a choice between unemployment and inflation he was prepared to choose inflation. He had shown great vision by saying during a visit to South Africa that the 'winds of change' were blowing through the continent with the rise of African Nationalism – and implied sympathy with the winds. Contrary to the evidence of his turgid memoirs, he was capable of producing crisp political statements. He described problems with a resigning treasury team as 'little local difficulties' – though he would have preferred not to be stuck with his 'never had it so good' statement.

He was a wonderful target for cartoonists with his moustache and swept back hair. His gift of showmanship combined with a rather patrician so-called Edwardian manner enabled Vicky to portray him as 'the entertainer' (a reference to a quite different John Osborne character). Vicky's other portrayal of him as Supermac, intended to be ironic, was misunderstood by some readers as representing his real view of Macmillan.

Do we all sell out in the end?

This characteristically scathing cartoon by Gerald Scarfe depicts Harold Wilson, who became a Knight of the Garter on his resignation in 1976. Harold Wilson became a Life Peer in 1985. Attlee was the only Labour Prime Minister to become an Earl.

Profile

An extremely bright economist, Harold Wilson (1916–1995), became a temporary Civil Servant during the Second World War, an MP in 1945 and almost immediately gained his first Ministerial appointment. What may in every sense be described as the twists and turns of his political career first became evident when he resigned with Nye Bevan largely over health service cuts in 1951. He subsequently attracted the support of Bevan's followers, retaining a leftwing reputation long after he was entitled to it if indeed he ever was. He stood against Hugh Gaitskell as Leader of the Labour Party during that party's agonies over nuclear disarmament (on which his own views were confusing). Following Gaitskell's premature death in 1963 he was elected Leader and became Prime Minister in 1964. He can be applauded for his skill in holding the Government together with a tiny majority from 1964 to 1966, and for his electioneering skill in 1964 and 1966. He can be condemned for not devaluing the currency in 1964 and for a wholly lack lustre campaign in 1970. When he did devalue in 1967 he made the misleading comment that 'The pound here in Britain in your pocket or purse or in your bank has not been devalued.' He was proof of the proposition in relation to his own party that 'Just because you are paranoid it does not mean that there is no one out to get you.' His Governments were bedevilled by the contrast between traditional socialist rhetoric and the actual requirements of governments faced with huge economic pressures.

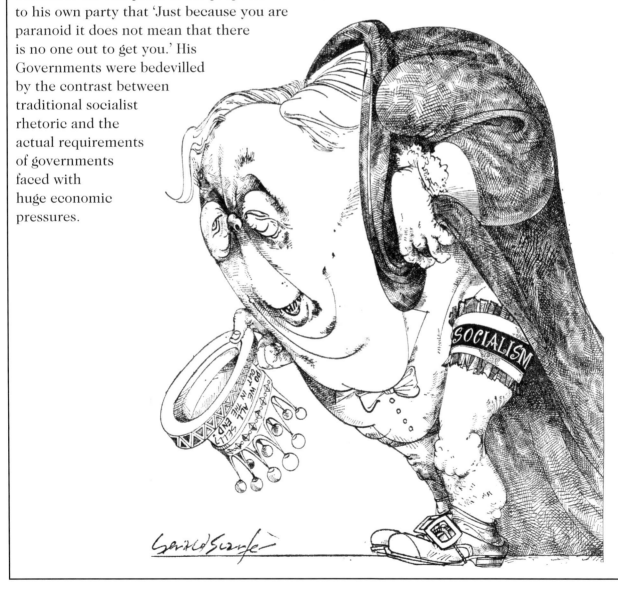

"I AM BIG. IT'S THE PICTURES THAT GOT SMALL."
(SUNSET BOULEVARD)

'I Am Big It's The Pictures That Got Small'

Garland's 1993 cartoon has Margaret Thatcher in the Gloria Swanson role from the film *Sunset Boulevard*, protesting against the European agreement reached by John Major.

Profile

Margaret Thatcher (1925–) was the daughter of a lower middle class shopkeeper in Grantham. After a degree in science she qualified as a lawyer and in 1959 became an MP. Cartoonists seized on the hat she wore at Conservative conferences, later as Secretary of State for Education she was criticised as 'Margaret Thatcher milk snatcher' for removing the privilege of free milk from some school children. In 1969 she said 'No woman in my time will be prime minister or chancellor or foreign secretary. Anyway I wouldn't want to be Prime Minister. You have to give yourself 100%.' In 1975 she challenged Edward Heath as Leader of the Conservative Party in opposition and beat him. (Relationships between them which had been cool to frosty now became wholly frozen.)

Perceptions of her achievements and failures as Prime Minister are familiar enough at the time of writing this book not to need detailed recapitulation. A major achievement was of course to be the first woman leader of a major political party, and then the first woman prime minister in the UK in 1979. She famously stood up for British interests as she saw them particularly in relation to Europe. She was forced out of office in 1990 by a combination of colleagues disaffected by her personal behaviour and disbelief that she would be able to lead them to yet another election victory (which would have been her fourth in a row). She did not go gently into retirement, and continued to offer her views, often in fairly strident language, on major issues. As with most modern politicians, it is not always clear whether the words she spoke were her own – but they were a gift for cartoonists. 'You turn if you want. This lady's not for turning.' 'There is no such thing as society'. Cartoonists did not capture Mitterand's description of her 'The eyes of Caligula, but the mouth of Marilyn Monroe.'

David Pitt

This cartoon by Sallon shows the first black peer after Learie Constantine (see Chapter 11).

Profile

Born in Grenada, David Pitt (1913–1994) came to Britain in 1932 and developed his career here for most of his subsequent life. He was a doctor in general practice for thirty years, and as a politician served for example on public bodies dealing with immigrants, community relations and was Chairman of Shelter the housing organisation. Pitt served on the London County Council when it was a significant body, and stood several times for Parliament including winnable seats without success. Race was a major factor in his final attempt in 1970 (as it apparently was in a later contest by the subsequent Lord Taylor in Cheltenham for the Conservative Party). He was London's first black magistrate, and after his final failure to become an MP he was given a peerage by Harold Wilson in 1975.

6

Army and Navy

Peerages developed initially either as a recognition of the landed power of the class immediately under the monarch, or as a recognition by the monarch of services rendered. The prosecution of war at sea or on land was one of the most obvious of those services – in the earliest days of course land battles fought between competing claimants for power and territory in England. The elevation of John Churchill to the Peerage as the 1st Duke of Marlborough in recognition of his successful campaigns on the continent of Europe was especially unusual since it was accompanied by, in effect, the gift of Blenheim Palace. However he preceded the evolution of cartoons and caricature (though

A Wellington Boot

As already mentioned in Chapter 3, this cartoon by Paul Pry (William Heath) is an example of a cartoon of allusion because it emphasises the eponymous boot as much as it does Wellington's face with its prominent hooked nose. It was published in 1827 when he was Commander in Chief of the Army.

Profile

Arthur Wellesley (1769–1852) got his first military experience in India, but gained his main reputation in the Peninsula War against France, waged in Spain and Portugal. He is unique amongst modern British soldiers in surviving a court of enquiry in 1809, for not fully exploiting a victory. The main military highlight however was not his successful continuous campaigns, but the final defeat of Napoleon at the Battle of Waterloo in 1815. It is unlikely he ever did say that the battle was won on the playing fields of Eton. It is more likely that he did actually say 'Publish and be damned' in relation to a blackmail threat – which has some relevance to the work of cartoonists. Successively Viscount, Earl, Marquess and

A WELLINGTON BOOT
Or the Head of the Armye   Pub by Tho.ˢ McLean 26 Haymarket London

finally Duke, he became a reluctant Premier in 1828. He carried Catholic Emancipation through despite his own inclinations, but then found the public which had adored him turned on him when he opposed parliamentary reform. He was used to command, not to persuade.

his successor the 5th Duke of Marlborough appears in Chapter 4).

Large sums of money were given to Wellington and to Nelson's heirs. The genius of generals and admirals was less clear in the two World Wars; titles were provided but much less money.

It is interesting to note that all the peerages shown through cartoon in this chapter are those of original creations. Military success does not seem to follow hereditary lines. Indeed it could be argued that it was the hereditary peers who helped to make the Crimean War in the 1860s, and especially the Charge of the Light Brigade, so costly in deaths.

Extirpation

This cartoon by Gillray refers to the victory in 1798 by the British fleet commanded by Horatio Nelson at Aboukir Bay over the French at the mouth of the Nile. Although Nelson had contributed to earlier victories such as Cape St Vincent in the previous year, Aboukir was the victory which he won by a daring manoeuvre. The cartoon shows that he had lost his right arm, but is not so clear in showing that he had lost an eye also.

Profile

Horatio Nelson (1758–1805) was created Baron as a result of his victory in 1798, and elevated to Viscount in 1801. On 21 October 1805 he fought the great battle off Cape Trafalgar which gave him his most lasting fame. He did not live to see his fleet victorious, as he was shot on his ship HMS Victory.

In public memory he is associated with the signal he flew at Trafalgar 'England expects that every man will do his duty', the coincidence of his death and the victory, and his involvement with Lady Hamilton. This latter was dramatised in a film starring Laurence Olivier and Vivien Leigh.

Extirpation of the Plagues of Egypt;–Destruction of Revolutionary Crocodiles;–or–The British Hero cleansing ỹ Mouth of ỹ Nile.

'Bobs'

This cartoon published in *Vanity Fair* on 21 June 1900 shows Field Marshall Lord Roberts against a rocky background which in fact on the right hand side depicts Kruger the leader of the Boer uprising.

Profile

Like all British generals of his time Lord Roberts (1832–1914) had learned his trade fighting in India – in his case especially successfully in Afghanistan. He eventually became Commander in Chief in India, and was made Baron in recognition of this. Early failures by the British Army in South Africa caused him to be sent there in 1899 to fight the Boers. He changed the military policy to make the army much more mobile, and returned to England and an Earldom. He died in France on active service having returned from retirement to serve with Indian troops.

Kitchener

This cartoon by Max Beerbohm (© Estate of Max Beerbohm) makes Kitchener look military although he is actually in civilian clothes.

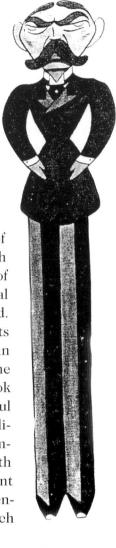

Profile

Lord Kitchener of Khartoum was most identified with the war in the Sudan, and the Battle of Omdurman in 1898 which led to the reoccupation of Khartoum where General Gordon had famously died. He took over from Roberts as Commander in Chief in South Africa to run the Boer War in 1900, and took it through to its successful conclusion. However military success was accompanied by a scorched earth policy and the internment of civilians in 'concentration' camps, in which large numbers died.

In 1914 he was appointed Secretary of State for War at the outbreak of hostilities. He had two major successes there. The first was to plan for at least a three year war rather than encouraging the 'home before Christmas' euphoria which initially occurred. His second success was to appear on a poster 'Your country needs you' with his own face and beckoning finger. This helped to create the large volunteer army through which the war was initially fought. The poster became an example for 'referential cartoons', which used the same style and finger. Margot Asquith said of him that although not a great man 'he made a great poster'. However he was contemptuous of politicians and obsessively secretive 'My colleagues tell military secrets to their wives, except Asquith, who tells them to other people's wives.' He was lost at sea on the way to Russia in 1916.

The Beatty Tilt

In this cartoon Bert Thomas illustrates the way Admiral David Beatty wore his cap which gave him additional recognition.

Profile

Admiral David Beatty (1871–1936) was the last publicly recognised dashing naval hero. This view has to be placed in context. The major naval battles he fought are still fought in books between protagonists of different views about whether the Germans or the British won – the general conclusion seems to be there was no conclusion. (Dogger Bank and Jutland). This Great War was the last in which rival navies sought to engage with each other on a massive scale in Europe. He was made an Earl in 1919, and awarded £100,000 by a grateful government.

Field Marshall Viscount Montgomery

Sallon's cartoon shows the two badge beret with which Montgomery defied normal rules about what generals should wear.

Profile

Montgomery of Alamein (1887–1976) learned from his own experiences as an officer in the First World War. He was especially concerned not to engage in what he described as 'more useless carnage'. He developed considerable popularity amongst his troops for this reason, although other generals particularly Americans with less experience of battles were inclined to criticise him for being too cautious. He achieved the first British success of the War at El Alamein in Egypt. He contributed to the successful planning and implementation of the Normandy landings, though his reputation was diminished by his ambitious plan which concluded in 'a bridge too far' at Arnhem. His military colleagues regarded him as a good boss and a very bad subordinate; the fact that he survived is a tribute to Eisenhower's skills and patience. He had an ego larger than even most military commanders. When asked after the war 'Who do you consider the three greatest generals of all time', his response was 'The other two were Alexander the Great and Napoleon'.

Douglas, Earl Haig

In this caricature Bert Thomas, through the concealing peak of Haig's hat, conveys a view of his subject as blinkered which coincides with that of many though not all historians.

Profile

Douglas Field Marshal Earl Haig (1861–1928) launched the campaigns on the Somme in 1916 and at Passchendele in 1917. In these campaigns huge number of British troops were lost, for tiny gains in ground. Haig did not think the war could be won anywhere other than France. Lloyd George who was appalled at the time, but could not remove him because of his political associations, took his revenge in his war memoirs. The main criticisms of him are that he continued these two battles long after it was clear they could not be won in the terms he sought. The other criticism is that he lived far behind the front lines, and had no contact with either his generals or with the appalling conditions faced by the ordinary troops there. His belief that he had divine support for this strategy was not proven. He was awarded an Earldom before major criticism of him became public. After the war he devoted himself to the interests of the soldiers who had fought for him, especially through the British Legion.

The Great Indian Governor Bird or Partition Pippit

In this 1948 cartoon Emmwood portrays a version of Mountbatten considerably different from the glamorous and successful war leader.

Profile

Earl Mountbatten of Burma (1900–1979) known as 'Dickie' was the son of Prince Louis Battenberg, forced to resign during World War I because of his German name. Untested in his peace time naval career, he was either unlucky or not very skilled as Captain of the Destroyer Kelly which was eventually sunk. This later enhanced his reputation in a rather odd way, because it was made the subject of a film *In Which We Serve* by Noel Coward. His first major effort as Chief of Combined Operations was a landing at Dieppe. This was a great failure and, because of the loss of Canadian troops, probably caused a vendetta subsequently run against Mountbatten by Beaverbrook and his newspapers. He became Supreme Commander Southeast Asia and was made a Viscount at the end of the Japanese War. His appointment as the last Viceroy of India with the remit to assist in the independence of India was adventurous and was as successful as circumstances allowed. His service career concluded with his role as Chief of the Defence Staff, and his public reputation was enhanced through television programmes which he fronted about himself. Described by Harold Wilson as 'the Shop Steward of Royalty', he contributed to the decision to change the name of the Royal Family to Mountbatten-Windsor.

Margaret Thatcher's survival of the IRA bomb in Eastbourne meant that the assassination of Mountbatten by the IRA made him the most prominent figure assassinated by them.

7

Lords and Ladies of Stage and Screen

While the House of Commons has been described as the theatre of politics (as well as a cockpit), a theatrical element is more visible in many respects in the House of Lords. This appears in the robes they wear on formal occasions especially the opening of the Parliamentary Session, in which the Monarch lowers herself to appear in the House of Lords but requires the Commons to be brought to her.

Although it could be argued that a number of Lords and Ladies have performed in a theatrical way, this chapter is concerned with the more restricted definition of those who have been involved in the Theatre or Film. It is notable that only one actor – Olivier – has been ennobled. While in one sense this could be seen as a recognition of his uniqueness as actor and manager of the National Theatre, it is interesting to see his isolated award compared with those for various impresarios who figure here.

In a chapter focused on the world of 'make believe', it seemed appropriate to include at least one fictional character – Lady Bracknell.

Gertie Millar

This is really an ordinary drawing rather than a cartoon, it has been included because of a particular period of the history of the peerage.

Profile
Gertie Millar Countess of Dudley (1879–1967) was one of George Edwarde's gaiety girls, the daughter of a millworker. She was a dancer with what was described as a small sweet voice. Her great successes were *The Quaker girl* (1910) and *Our Miss Gibbs*. Her last stage appearance was in *Flora* in 1918. She married the 2nd Earl of Dudley in 1924, and represents a change in the traditional aristocratic view of actresses who might be mistresses, but not wives. Other stage stars who married into the peerage included Rosie Boote who married the Marquess of Headfort and Tilly Losch who married the Earl of Caernarfon.

Lady Diana Cooper

Sallon's caricature of Diana Cooper does not show her as one of the most beautiful women of her time.

Profile

In contrast to Gertie Millar, Lady Diana Cooper (Viscountess Norwich) (1892–1986) only had one major stage success, when she appeared in *The Miracle* a play without words by Max Reinhardt in 1923. She played the Madonna through into the 1930s both in London and in Broadway. She was a daughter of the 8th Duke of Rutland. Famous as a hostess and society figure, she married Alfred Duff Cooper who became Viscount Norwich. In her capacity as a hostess she was tested as his wife when he was Ambassador in Paris. Ernest Bevin as Foreign Secretary made 'violent advances' to her in 1946. She rejected his offer of 'One sweet night of bliss at the Dorchester Hotel.'

Viscount Chandos

This caricature by Felix Topolski was published in 1961, when Chandos had left political life and returned to his business role as Chairman of the then Associated Electrical Industries.

Profile

Viscount Chandos (Oliver Lyttleton) (1893–1972) is included in this chapter because he was a major fundraiser and first Chairman of the National Theatre from 1962–1971. Although he had some disagreements with Olivier as Director of the National Theatre especially over the production of a play which Chandos thought traduced the memory of Winston Churchill, he was a crucial figure in carrying through the development of the NT. Given that one of the two major theatre spaces at the NT should be named after him, it is appropriate as a Conservative that it was the traditional proscenium arch stage which was named as the Lyttleton.

The Baron Olivier of Brighton

In this caricature Clive Francis shows Olivier in his role as Edgar in *The Dance of Death*. This, rather than Othello or Richard III was selected because it was in this role that Olivier says 'I received an exceedingly kind and giddy making letter from the Prime Minister Harold Wilson inviting me to accept a peerage.'

Profile

Laurence Olivier's (1907–1989) setting up of the NT at the Old Vic, while still performing in major stage roles was extraordinary. Theatrical historians emphasise the extent to which he revolutionised the style of acting. He was bold, daring 'of the earth earthy', particularly in his difference in both style and roles from his great contemporary John Gielgud. The sardonic resonance and shock inflections he used in his delivery were easily imitated. He grabbed the attention of audiences – though some members were sometimes shocked by what they saw as caricature in the case of particularly Othello and Shylock. His magnificence was represented by the fact that all other actors including Gielgud and Richardson were measured against him.

Bernard Delfont

Griffin shows in this cartoon for the *Daily Mirror* Delfont as a dancer – his early career.

Profile

Born Boris Vinogradsky Bernard Delfont (1909–1994) came to England with his two brothers in 1911. (They took the name Grade). He changed his name when he took up his short career as a stage dancer. His main fame was as a producer and impresario on stage, on film and then on TV. He represents an important part of the theatre, that of creating the finance which enables playwrights and actors to be heard. He was also responsible for many years for the filming of the Royal Variety Performance for television, which was more of a major television event then than now.

Sidney Bernstein

Marc's economic lines show a man of determination.

Profile

The fact that Sidney Bernstein (1899–1993), who was made a Life Peer in 1989, was both a socialist and a millionaire was understandably seen as paradoxical. He developed a chain of Granada cinemas in the 1930s which tended to be both large and full of exotic décor. His main fame rests however on the development of Granada Television, when ITV was set up in competition with the previous monopoly holders at the BBC. One of the programmes he sponsored, *Coronation Street*, still exists. The other forms he favoured, drama and high quality journalism through for example *World in Action*, have not survived at such a visibly high level.

LEW GRADE PRESENTS MOSES

'How come Moses has got a bigger billing than I have?'

Jak, the *Evening Standard* cartoonist, created major difficulties for his paper with his portrayal of striking electricians and terrorism addicted Irish people. Here the presentation of Grade's ever-present huge cigar has a companion in Lew Grade's nose.

Profile
Lord Lewis Grade (1906–1998), who became Lew, arrived from Odessa with his brother who became Bernard Delfont. He was given a peerage at the same time as Delfont in 1976. Also like Delfont he was originally a dancer – he was a world champion dancer of the Charleston. He became an impresario largely after 1945 with television and then films. His films increasingly became of the mega variety, and included perhaps paradoxically for a Jew *Jesus of Nazareth*.

Lord Richard Attenborough

Attenborough developed an exaggerated reputation as someone who cried at public occasions, so cartoonists frequently drew him with tears streaming. Clive Francis is more respectful.

Profile

Lord Richard Attenborough (1923–) originally acquired fame as a film actor, particularly in *Brighton Rock* as a terrorising cruel Pinkie, and later as a less than brave seaman in Noel Coward's *In Which We Serve*. Although primarily a film director he still continues to act for example in *Jurassic Park*. His film credits as director include *Oh What a Lovely War*, *A Bridge too Far*, and *Gandhi* (which collected many Oscars) and *Cry Freedom*.

Jamie Lee Curtis

The cartoon by Gary refers to the fact that Curtis had said publicly there was nothing wrong with revealing her body as it was in her mid forties, and that other women should similarly feel free.

Profile

Jamie Lee Curtis (1958–) the American film actress is married to Christopher Haden-Guest 5th Baron. Herself the daughter of a sort of film aristocracy (Tony Curtis and Janet Leigh), her major films include *A Fish called Wanda*, *Trading Places* and *Blue Steel*. It is the case that she had earlier in her career revealed much more of her physical self than was normal in the wives of peers – which may have explained her pleasure later in putting on the robes of a Peeress for the opening of Parliament.

The classless society the 1997 model

This cartoon by Martin Rowson refers to the award of a peerage by Prime Minister John Major to Andrew Lloyd Webber.

Profile

The depiction of Lord Andrew Lloyd Webber (1948–) overwhelmed within his role is a more traditional cartoonists' view than the grotesque version of John Major. While there has been criticisms of Lloyd Webber on musical grounds, it is not clear why he should be accused of lack of taste. He has been immensely successful with his productions including *Joseph and the Amazing Technicolour Dreamcoat*, *Cats*, *Evita* and the *Phantom of the Opera*. As one commentator said, 'anyone who could write the masterpiece *Joseph* which has sustained millions of families on dozens of motorways the length and breadth of Britain deserves to be honoured'.

A handbag?

Clive Francis drew Judi Dench as Lady Bracknell, a role she performed at the National Theatre in 1982.

Profile

Lady Bracknell (1895–) was created by Oscar Wilde in his play *The Importance of Being Earnest*. Whereas Maudie Littlehampton was seen by millions regularly in the *Daily Express*, Lady Bracknell has been seen by thousands on the stage and screen. Oscar Wilde gave her the two words which have become the most famous and most imitated of any offered by a Lady on stage and screen. This was her incredulous response to the news that the man who wants to become engaged to her niece Cecily was found as a baby in a handbag in a railway carriage. The tremulous horror with which Dame Edith Evans visited these words was so distinctive that apart from mimics subsequent performers in the role have tried to avoid copying her. The two current great British actresses Dame Maggie Smith and Dame Judi Dench have created quite different portrayals.

8

Press, Radio and TV

As already noted the first influx of people clearly from 'business' started in the 1880s. 1895 saw the arrival of the first of what became a long sequence of 'Press Lords'. This was Algernon Borthwick, perhaps a more memorable name than that of his Peerage as Lord Glenesk. The more significant elevations were those of Edward Levy-Lawson the proprietor of the *Daily Telegraph* in 1903 who became Lord Burnham, and in 1905 Alfred Harmsworth became Lord Northcliffe. The Astors of American origin originally ennobled largely through political donations diverted into newspaper ownership at different stages of the *Times* and *Observer*. Beaverbrook, after Northcliffe by far the most famous of them all, was a Canadian. It is difficult to identify a significant newspaper owner who was not given a Peerage. (More recently emphasis was turned at least by Margaret Thatcher to giving Knighthoods to editors.)

The precipitating factor clearly was the development of mass circulation newspapers particularly through Northcliffe's *Daily Mail*. Their potential for political influence, or alternatively a view of them as public

Wanted a Man

Will Dyson the great socialist cartoonist for the *Daily Herald* drew this cartoon when Alfred Harmsworth, the first Lord Northcliffe was at the peak of his direct influence on the conduct of the war.

Profile

Lord Northcliffe (1855–1922) had founded the popular press in Britain on 4th May 1896 with his new paper the *Daily Mail*. It sold 400,000 copies and he exclaimed 'We've struck a goldmine.' He came to dominate Fleet Street then the centre of Newspaper publishing – known colloquially as 'The Street of Shame'. He ran campaigns about munitions in the early stages of the First World War. Undoubtedly a megalomaniac, there were suggestions that his mental faculties were deranged. His instructions to one of his other papers, the *Times*, became more and more bizarre.

educators, provided the occasion. The latter point was much more evident and certainly put in justification for recognition of highly visible people first on Radio, and then on Television. The BBC became a part of that not entirely mythical creature 'The Establishment'.

Recognition of the power of the press was given in critical form by Rudyard Kipling, who summed up Beaverbrook's political standpoint as 'power without responsibility: the prerogative of the harlot throughout the ages'. His cousin Stanley Baldwin, less likely to know about harlots than some Prime Ministers, used the phrase in 1931 when under attack by the *Mail* and *Express*. It has subsequently become a cliché about the press in general.

'I tell yer the papers aren't up yet'

This cartoon by Low shows all the major owners of the press were literally 'press barons' – Beaverbrook, Rothermere, Kemsley, Camrose and Layton. The Royal Commission into the British Press in 1947 was the first to look openly at the ownership, structure and purposes of the press. Beaverbrook in evidence said directly that his papers pursued his political agenda.

Eating People is Wrong

The two cartoons of Beaverbrook present totally different views of him, which makes them especially interesting and justifies this double inclusion. The first gentle cartoon is by his own cartoonist Cummings in the *Daily Express*, the second by the independent Timothy Birdsall. Birdsall's cartoon refers to the fact that he was a great seducer of people; he charmed for example the socialists Nye Bevan and Michael Foot.

Profile

Max Aitken, Lord Beaverbrook (1879–1964) came to this country from Canada already a millionaire. He moved into Conservative politics, but accepted to his subsequent regret a Peerage in 1916 and necessarily left the House of Commons. His view was that 'The House of Lords is the British Outer Mongolia for retired politicians.' His political engagement in the First World War as Minister of Information, and in the Second in several jobs under Churchill showed both his ingenuity and his incapacity to stick at political work for very long. He used his papers as political weapons in favour of Empire Free Trade, against Baldwin. He undoubtedly enjoyed stirring things up but this sometimes included (despite the protestations of his biographer A J P Taylor) vendettas against particular individuals such as Lord Mountbatten.

John Reith

Low's cartoon wonderfully presents one aspect of John Reith's view of himself 'Everything over 6´ 2″ is an affliction'.

Profile

John Lord Reith (1889–1971) was the founder of the BBC in the sense of its existence as a publicly funded organisation, which was intended to be independent of straightforward politics, and to set some kind of higher cultural purpose than many daily newspapers. He ran the BBC from 1922 to 1938, and set a tone which has echoes today. He moved into Government during the Second World War and then had a variety of public appointments. As he confessed to the interviewer John Freeman however he rarely felt that he was 'stretched'. He was an example of a man whose capabilities were great but whose ambitions were often misdirected.

WHAT HAS BEEN CANADA'S MOST IMPORTANT EXPORT TO BRITAIN? ☐ Newsprint? ☐ Toilet Paper? ☐ ROY THomSon?

Lord Thomson

This cartoon is by Aislin (Terry Mosher) a Canadian cartoonist. It comments on his ownership of the *Times*. He was in fact a benign, non-interfering owner.

Profile

Lord Thomson of Fleet (1894–1971) built on his success with radio stations and newspapers in Canada and moved into the United Kingdom. Initially he invested in television, describing a franchise as 'a licence to print money'. Under him the *Sunday Times* began its progress towards dominating the heavy Sunday market. The *Times* which he acquired later gave him huge problems with the unions and were leading to a constant financial drain. Both papers were subsequently acquired by the Australian Rupert Murdoch, who led them into a more strident support of Conservative policies than Thomson had followed.

Lord Rees Mogg

Nicola's view of Lord Rees Mogg for the *Guardian* emphasises either wariness or weariness.

Profile

Lord William Rees Mogg (1928–) acquired his main reputation as Editor of the *Times* from 1967 to 1981. Subsequently he was Vice Chairman of the BBC, and Chairman of the Arts Council from 1982–1989 during which time he was given his Peerage in 1988. These three appointments in many ways represent the British establishment at work, with its identification of 'the great and the good'. He continues as a columnist for the *Times*; the imminent collapse of capitalism which he forecast in 1991 has not yet occurred.

Dr Charles Hill

Hill is shown by Ted Harrison with the sort of bag doctors used to carry – not a handbag.

Profile

Charles Hill (1904–1989) First an ordinary doctor, then a spokesman for the medical profession, he acquired fame first as 'The Radio Doctor', offering easy to understand advice on basic medical matters. He referred for example to the prune as 'that black coated worker'. He led the bargaining with Nye Bevan the Minister of Health about the introduction of the National Health Service, moved into government in 1951 and served under Churchill, Eden and Macmillan. His voice was distinctive – deep, rich and authoritative without being patronising. He was later given the unique distinction of being Chairman of first the Independent Television Authority and then the BBC.

Lord Rothermere

In this cartoon for the *Sunday Times*, Rothermere's involvement in the *Mail* newspapers is indicated. This caricature was drawn by Gary in 1997 at a time when he was defying all past family precedent and his own previous views by suggesting that Labour would be a more effective government than the Conservatives.

Profile

Vere Harmsworth Lord Rothermere (1925–2002) was the effective owner of the *Daily Mail*, which came to him via Northcliffe's brother Harmsworth. He had provided the initiative, through effective selection of some very good editors, for first the recovery of the *Daily Mail*, and then its success in overtaking its rival the *Daily Express*. He was certainly less reactionary in his political views than his father in the 1930s. He was also more successful as son of previous Harmsworths and Rothermeres than was Max Aitken the son of Lord Beaverbrook.

Melvyn Bragg

Nicola drew this in association with Bragg's birthday in October 2002; the emphasis on his hair is unusual.

Profile

Lord Bragg (1939–). He has had an extraordinarily productive career as author and broadcaster. His novels, particularly the most recent dealing with family life in the Second World War, had the advantage of dealing with recognisable families through interesting but believable situations. As a broadcaster he presents one of the longest running shows (other than *Coronation Street*) on ITV – *The Southbank Show*. This has survived as a mainly highbrow event on a Sunday night, when the BBC's equivalent programme totally disappeared.

The BBC

In this cartoon Gary shows John Birt the Director General of the BBC, and his Chairman Duke Hussey taking the padlocks off the BBC when its charter was renewed in 1994.

Profile

John Birt (1944–) moved from the ITV network to become First Deputy Director General and then Director General of the BBC. His tenure of office was criticised at the time as being too much addicted to managerialism, to domination by financial issues instead of creative issues, and an inability to get some of his staff to work successfully with him. However he was successful in securing the future of the BBC through its charter which would not have been possible without his demonstrative revolution which fitted in with the then Conservative Government philosophy. He became an adviser to the Labour Government on subjects of prisons and crime, and transport on which it had not previously been recognised that he was at all knowledgeable.

Profile

Lord Hussey (1923–). Hussey reveals in his biography that although he had greatly favoured Birt's appointment, he finished by being disappointed with him. The apparent comradeship in the cartoon is therefore probably misleading. He served with distinction in the Second World War, and showed great bravery and fortitude in recovering from the amputation of a leg. He had been a top executive on Times Newspapers and was heavily involved in the shutdown of the *Times* as it tried to defeat Trade Unions. Before he was offered the job of Chairman of the BBC in 1986 he said to a friend 'They'll be hard pushed to persuade some idiot to take it on.' He served there for ten years and perhaps as a result of that experience said 'I have always enjoyed being thought a fool – at least not to be clever. It gives you an immediate advantage over those around you.' He was called 'Duke', but this was an abbreviation of Marmaduke not a title (see also Duke Ellington, Count Basie and Earl Hines).

9

Business

One of the great changes in the composition of the Peerage occurred when men were ennobled who were not either heroes of war nor already significant landowners. Other forms of justification, such as high position in the Civil Service, service overseas as Viceroys, and finally the acquisition of wealth through business provided a justification.

In the 20th Century the association originally drawn between philanthropic activity and a Peerage, already breached by a more accurate association between a donation to a party and a Peerage, became more confused. Some businessmen acquired Peerages because of their diligence and good reputation as business people. Some acquired it because they were well known business people who contributed to a political party (or 'persuaded' their companies to make donations). The following cartoons are not a representative sample of any of these categorisations, but are included because of intrinsic interest.

Alfred the Peacemaker

This cartoon by Matt (Sandford) was drawn when Alfred Mond had led a conference achieving agreement between employers and trade unionists.

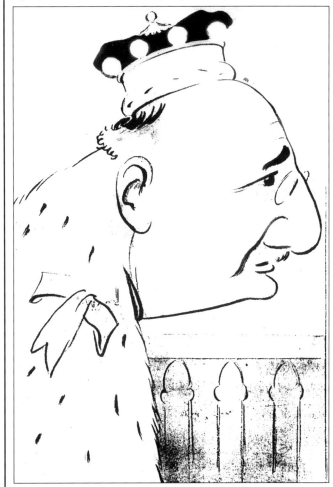

Profile

Alfred Mond, 1st Lord Melchett (1868–1930), was born in Lancashire as the son of a German born Jew who set up the original chemicals business in which Alfred developed management skills. By the standards of his time he was an innovative leader. His initial interests were in organisation and research; he turned towards championing processes of rationalisation and amalgamation, and finally achieved significant fame again unusual for his time in trying to develop closer co-operation between employers and the people they employed. On the one hand he was emphatically against lock outs and strikes, on the other hand he believed in profit sharing and employee shareholding. His amalgamations eventually resulted in the development of the huge firm, Imperial Chemical Industries. His political contributions were less significant, first as a Liberal MP and then later as a Tory MP.

Lord Leverhulme

The frock coat and spats were more typical for industrialists than the check bow tie in Matt's cartoon.

Profile

Like Mond, W H Lever, 1st Viscount Leverhulme (1851–1925) was born in Lancashire. His initial claim to fame was the development of Sunlight Soap and, subsequently the physical development of the site Port Sunlight. Like Mond, he worked through amalgamations as his original business proved successful. He had a brief spell as a Liberal MP for three years from 1906. Again like Mond he was concerned for his workers, in his case focusing more on the planning of relatively pleasant houses and gardens for their domestic environment. He created a hugely successful business, which later mutated into Unilever.

Richard Beeching

In Sallon's cartoon for the *Daily Mirror* in November 1963 during his reorganisation of the railways, Beeching is shown as a guard signalling that a train should move forward.

Profile

Richard, Lord Beeching (1913–1985), known mainly as Dr Beeching from his PhD in physics had a successful career in ICI, where he reached the main board as Technical Director. His success there led to his appointment first to look at the operation of railways, and then to direct them as Chairman of the (nationalised) British Railways Board. Nationalisation of the railways after the Second World War had provided no easy solution to efficiency and cost – any more than privatisation did in the 1990s. His name became synonymous with a massive reduction in the number of railway lines, trains and stations. Although he held other senior positions in industry, it was his involvement in the railways which led to his fame. Beeching was in some ways a repetition of the phenomenon of an industrialist brought in to attack public costs – like Sir Eric Geddes in 1921.

Arnold Weinstock

This cartoon for the *Times* in July 2002 looked back at the cash mountain Weinstock built for GEC – which disappeared by the time he died.

Profile

While the start to Arnold Weinstock's (1924–2002) managerial career may have been aided by being the husband of the daughter of an industrialist in electrical engineering, once he had entered the boardroom his progress was due to his own skills and attitudes. He was the Managing Director of the General Electric Company from 1963–1996, during which time he not only made major successes in the development of his own original companies, but acquired other and sometimes larger electrical companies such as English Electric and transformed them also. His philosophy of management was to have a very small central headquarters, and focus attention in immense detail on 'the bottom line' for each of his companies. The great financial success of his business led to what turned out to be a great irony. He was heavily criticised for sitting on 'a mountain of cash', and not reinvesting it by diversifying into other businesses. He must have been mortified before his death by the efforts of his predecessors who managed to change the name of the business, to diversify, and to lose huge amounts of money.

Tory Donor

The 'donor' in Nicola's *Guardian* cartoon of 22 August 1996 is Lord Saatchi. The financing of political parties was in the news – again.

Profile

Maurice Saatchi (1946–) with his brother was the founder in 1970 of what became the most famous advertising company in the UK. He was Chairman from 1985–1994. The Saatchis developed forms of advertising, and modern styles of communication both to get contracts and then to carry them out. While it is not necessary for advertising and PR companies to believe in the products of their clients, Saatchi was heavily involved in the presentation of the policies of the Conservative Party. One of the advertisements for which he was said to be responsible portrayed Tony Blair with devil's eyes. This was largely unsuccessful but has relevance in a book of cartoons because it became the basis for quite a lot of the cartoons. When he received his Peerage in 1996 objections were raised that Maurice Saatchi had not only worked for the Conservative Party through his advertising agency, but had actually been a major donor. His agency provided the Tories with 'Labour isn't working' in 1978/79, which was successful as an advertisement and also spawned a number of cartoons.

10

Sporting Peers

It is not surprising that cricket predominates amongst the cartoons of sporting Peers selected. It has had a longer and stronger association with Peers than any sport except perhaps racing. Some Peers who might have been included here appear in other sections. Alec Douglas-Home, then Lord Dunglass, went on a minor tour with the MCC. He is the only Prime Minister to have played at a serious level of cricket – though it is often presumed that John Major would have liked to have done so.

The Liberal Prime Minister the Earl of Rosebery might have been included as a successful racehorse owner, but this would have been unduly perverse in terms of selection. In the reverse direction, a cartoon of Lord Seb Coe engaging in judo as William Hague's personal assistant would have been a poor memorial to his career as one of the world's greatest athletes.

Lord Lonsdale

This cartoon shows Lonsdale in jolly mood – as do several other cartoonists.

Profile

Fifth Earl Lonsdale (1857–1944) had three major sporting interests. One of his horses won the St Leger in 1922, but otherwise he was unsuccessful in racing. He raised the standards in boxing, and was the originator of the 'Lonsdale belt' acquired by British champions. He also raced yachts. Perhaps not surprisingly, he did not pay as much attention to the management of his estates or to the management of his finances in general. He was known as the 'Yellow Earl' because his carriages and livery were in that colour.

Lord Harris

This cartoon in *Vanity Fair*, was only the second of a cricketer in that journal, following W G Grace.

Profile

Lord Harris (1851–1933) was remarkable not so much for his personal capacity as a cricketer, although he played for Kent for many years, and also captained England – indeed he captained in the first Test at the Oval in 1880. He held important and sustained office in the MCC, and exercised a sometimes autocratic control over many aspects of the game. He helped significantly for example with the attack on throwing by bowlers in the 1880s. Harris played much of his cricket wearing brown boots – a phenomenon the compiler of this book encountered himself when playing against a team at Eton in the 1950s.

Yorkshire Cricket

In the colour version of this cartoon for *Vanity Fair*, Hawke's striped blazer is actually in the colours of the I Zingari Club, not the blazer of Yorkshire.

Profile

Lord Hawke (1860–1938), Captain of Yorkshire from 1881 until 1910, and with a continuing involvement until his death in 1938 Hawke's career had significant parallels with that of Lord Harris. In his case he is remembered for the way in which he ruled his professionals. While being conscientious about their income – he introduced winter pay – he dismissed some of them who were addicted to alcohol. Yorkshire were champion county eight times during his captaincy. The *Dictionary of National Biography* does not include the most famous remark he ever made 'I trust no professional ever captains England'. Apologists later claimed that this referred to his fear about the disappearance of the amateur cricketer, rather than his aversion to professionals.

IMPERIAL WELCOME

Imperial Welcome

Low's cartoon refers to the occasion in 1943 when the West Indian cricketer Learie Constantine was refused admission to an hotel. At that time Constantine was at the end of a cricket career which had blazed with excitement.

Profile

Lord Learie Constantine was a fast bowler, a batsman who hit the ball very hard and to some amazing places – though with much less consistent success than all rounders like Botham and Sobers. Despite the impact of the event shown in the cartoon, Constantine had in fact overcome many aspects of the colour bar by playing professional cricket in Lancashire for ten years. He studied for the bar in the UK, and returned to Trinidad at first as a politician, and then as that country's High Commissioner in London. Exciting as he was to his contemporaries as a cricketer, his particular place in this book is due to the fact that he was appointed as the first black Life Peer in 1969. (He had stayed on in this country after his time as High Commissioner.)

" NOW, COLIN, WHEN YOU SEE THIS REARING SIZZLER ROARING TOWARDS YOUR OFF STUMP FROM THOMSON...!"

'Now Colin, when you see this rearing sizzler . . .'

The Australian cartoonist Norman Mitchell offers a humorous comment on the arrival of Colin Cowdrey for the England/Australia test series 1974–1975. Many of England's batsmen had been terrorised by the pace of Thomson and Lillee, and several had broken bones.

Profile
Lord Colin Cowdrey of Tonbridge (1932–2000) at the age of 42 was requested by the England Captain and management to make his sixth trip to a test series in Australia. His first appearance produced the perhaps apocryphal story that on arriving at the wicket he said to Thomson 'Good morning I don't think we've met, my name is Cowdrey'.

Cowdrey was a batsman about whom the word felicitous might have been invented. His style depended on timing rather than power, with the occasional consequence that he could be hemmed in if his timing and the nature of the batting pitch were not in harmony. He played in over 100 tests, 27 as Captain. The England selectors could not make up their mind about him as captain, where his ease of stroke play was not always matched by his decision making. He was given his Peerage in recognition of his subsequent services to the MCC and the International Cricket Council, in which roles his courtesy and diplomacy were both tested and successful.

11

Intellectuals

The field of choice for this section is rather small. This may not entirely be a surprise to those for whom the words 'intellectual' and 'Lord' would seem an unlikely association. The relatively small number of intellectual Lords is reduced further in terms of the selection available for this book because not many of them have become public figures who were also the subject of cartoons. It will also be noticed that of those featured here, only two (Bertrand Russell and Lord Rothschild) were hereditary peers; the others acquired their honours through public service.

Lord Cherwell

Sallon's cartoon captures the determination of Cherwell – and the days when Ulster Unionists were not the only people to wear bowler hats.

Profile

As Fred Lindemann, Lord Cherwell's (1886–1957) Oxford career as Professor of Physics was effectively taken over by his involvement with Winston Churchill. He agreed with Churchill on the issue of air power in the 1930s, and was subsequently employed by Churchill in various administrative jobs in his government. Churchill, like most politicians not educated or informed on scientific matters found Lindemann's capacity to explain complex scientific and economic problems in terms he could understand extremely useful. He had a leading role in helping to set up Britain's atomic programme. In a very different way he represents like Keynes and Rothschild a rare coincidence of high academic qualifications with the ability to influence politicians. He was a good hater of individuals in particular, and Germans in general. His own certainty of mind, based on his view of the scientific facts, was not always matched by an effective later outcome.

Noel Annan

This cartoon by Marc captures his bonhomie, but not his intellect. Annan reviewed a collection of cartoons by Marc, in which he contrasts Marc's cool appraisal with other cartoonists 'slashing and bashing away'.

Profile

Noel Annan (1916–2000) established his reputation first as an academic at Cambridge, with lectures of such novelty and colour in delivery that for example undergraduates came to lectures on sociology at 9 o'clock on a Saturday morning. He moved to UCL in 1956, and later was Vice Chancellor London University and then became a member of the 'great and good', invited to serve on committees and commissions, particularly one in 1977 on the BBC. In 1990 Annan published his explanation of the culture and political influences on himself and others in the 1930s and war period in a major book *Our Age*. Another book *The Dons* included a chapter on the 'Intellectual Aristrocracy' which provided no further names for this chapter.

Lord Clark

This cartoon by Ted Harrison emphasises the egg head intellectual aspect of Kenneth Clark.

Profile

Kenneth Clark's (1903 to 1983) career as for example the youngest director of the National Gallery at the age of thirty-one, and his studies of fine art would not have brought him national attention outside his small circle. His period as Chairman of the Arts Council, and even more controversially as first Chairman of the Independent Television Authority brought him more to the public eye. However his main public distinction came about through his television programme in 1969. Although the title *Civilisation* was misleading in that it focused entirely on Art, it was an unparalleled success, achieved through lucid prose. His son Alan acquired notoriety as a diarist.

"THE FELLER OUGHT TO BE ASHAMED! ENCOURAGING RAIN!"

'The Feller Ought to be Ashamed . . .'

Low's cartoon of January 1938 shows Maynard Keynes surveyed by Blimp (and Chamberlain and Simon).

Profile

John Maynard Keynes (1883–1946) was a man of widely varied cultural interests who managed to be both pre-eminent as an academic economist and also engaged in the practical application of his views. He disagreed with the decisions on frontiers and reparations at the 1919 Peace Conference. *The Economic Consequences of the Peace* was his first influential book. He became involved with Lloyd George who he had criticised harshly in 1919, but with whom he developed an association in the 1929 Liberal document *We can conquer unemployment*. Keynes attacked the dominant economic theories at the time of the Great Depression and large scale unemployment, developing his views on employment and the function of interest in his two major works *Treatise on Money* 1930 and *The General Theory* in 1936. He became the most famous figure in economic theory, and his views dominated economic policy particularly in the United States and Great Britain until the 1980s. His practical involvement resumed with the Bretton Woods Conference in 1944, which set up the International Monetary Fund and the International Bank. He also negotiated the Loan from the United States in 1945 which prevented what otherwise would have been an economic collapse in this country. Unlike many theorists he was successful both in actually working out economic policy, and at a personal level where he created a significant fortune; he left the equivalent today of £12m.

Thinks

Trog's cartoon in 1973 appeared when Lord Rothschild made an unapproved speech on Britain's future which he saw as more gloomy than Heath wanted to present.

Profile

Lord Victor Rothschild (1910 to 1990). He was originally a biologist, then a wartime bombs disposal expert; he was Research Co-ordinator for Shell when he took up a unique position in Government. While British prime ministers had for many years had advisers with special access to them, (Lord Hankey, Thomas Jones, and less admirably Horace Wilson who advised Neville Chamberlain) Edward Heath was the first British Prime Minister to set up a unit in 1970 specifically to think and work outside Civil Service departmental structures. Rothschild headed this innovation, formally called the Central Policy Review Staff, colloquially the Think Tank. His first volume of autobiography was entitled *Meditation of a Broomstick* and contained 3 cartoons about his Think Tank. In two he does not appear, and in the third he is a tiny figure.

Civil Disobedience

Bertrand Russell (and others) were so concerned about the threat of nuclear war, that they were prepared to break the law. Vicky's 1961 cartoon celebrates this.

Profile

Bertrand Russell (1872 to 1970) became third Earl in 1931. Although his work was not always regarded highly in the academic world, which was inevitably suspicious of someone who attempted in some of his books to translate philosophy into language understandable by a normally educated person, Russell wrote major works of academic significance as well as more popular books. However his great fame arose because of his involvement in the wider public world, with his resistance to World War I, and a six month prison sentence for sedition after the War. He became a major public figure after 1954 when he led first the Campaign for Nuclear Disarmament and then the more radical Committee of One Hundred. In 1961 at the age of 89 he served a week in prison as a result of his civil disobedience. His sharp rather raucous though upper class voice became familiar as did his rather beaky features. Russell's sexual adventures through his four wives and other women were never represented in cartoons about him.

Sidney Webb

Webb is drawn here by Nicolas Bentley in clothes appropriate to his role as Baron Passfield. (© Nicolas Bentley)

Profile

Sidney Webb, Lord Passfield (1859 to 1947) and his wife Beatrice Webb formed the most powerful pair of social reformers ever known in this country. He helped to form the Fabian Society, wrote a major essay in *Fabian Essays on Socialism*, made a major contribution to the Labour Party Manifesto in 1918. He became an MP in 1922 and served in the Labour Cabinets of 1924 and 1929. The Webbs' early books on the *History of Trade Unionism* 1894, and Sydney's service on the *Royal Commission on Trade Union Law* showed the serious work he put into books which broke fresh ground. They produced the phrase 'The inevitability of gradualness' which epitomised their approach to social reform, yet in the 1930s they produced an enthusiastic account of Stalinist Russia and Soviet Communism. This was a bizarrely different view to that of all their previous life. It was a strange coincidence that Webb, although thoroughly British in origin, looked like an elderly version of Lenin.

12

Ladies – Mostly Blessed

The familiar toast 'The Ladies – God bless them' is perhaps more likely to be seen nowadays as patronising rather than genuinely rewarding. Although it is difficult to believe that many of the individuals portrayed in this chapter might have been patronised, it is likely that all of them experienced some of the more ancient behaviours of males towards females. They have been given a separate chapter to highlight some of the more interesting personalities who might not otherwise appear. (The unique Baroness Thatcher appears in Chapter 6 as well as here).

Until the creation of Life Peerages in 1958, no women sat in the House of Lords. A few women achieved prominence as MPs. The first to be elected, though she never took her seat, was Countess Markiewicz – who gained her title from her Polish husband. The general rule, that those included must actually be holders of a Peerage rather than an honorary title is breached for Maudie, Lady Littlehampton. Maudie is a figure of such social significance in cartooning that she has been included.

The feud which developed between Asquith and Lloyd George, and their descendants was rather like the Montagues and Capulets. Margot Asquith, Violet Bonham-Carter and Megan Lloyd George form an interesting triptych. (Violet and Megan had honorary titles before becoming peeresses in their own right).

The Two Patriotic Duchesses

This cartoon by Rowlandson refers to an election in 1784 in the constituency of Westminster. It was one of the few before 1832 with a significant number of electors. Corruption – the purchasing of votes – was endemic. In this election the Duchesses of Devonshire and Portland engaged in what has been described as the most famous canvassing campaign in history on behalf of Charles James Fox. It was claimed that they both offered to kiss electors – though this may not actually have happened. Fox lost the election.

Royal Hobby's or the Hertfordshire Cockhorse

George Cruikshank (1819) shows Lady Hertford, Mistress of the Prince of Wales driving him on the then new vehicle the velocipede. The Prince was Regent during one of the several episodes of madness endured by his father George III. The sexual relationship is emphasised in the style of the drawing and also in the text 'I'll make you drive it home.' 'You shall remember pushing your hobby in Hertford'.

Isabella Marchioness of Hertford was the second wife of the 2nd Marquess. She was apparently intelligent and worldly, and probably sexually interesting enough for the Regent to pursue her successfully despite her married state. She influenced his political views.

The Fashionable Mamma, or the Convenience of Modern Dress

Gillray in 1796 satirises several fashions of the day. It portrays Lady Charlotte Campbell second daughter of the Duke of Argyll. The convenience of modern dress with a low and exposed bosom is part of the point, as is the extravagant feathered headdress. The apparent lack of interest by the mother in the proceedings is also clear.

The Fashionable Mamma, – or – The Convenience of Modern Dress

My Lady Astor

This cartoon by Nicolas Bentley© from the early 1930s shows Lady Astor in exactly the opposite mode of conduct which she was likely to adopt. She was an active proselytiser for temperance.

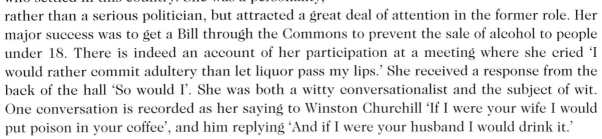

Profile

The election law was changed in 1918, women were allowed to become MPs as well as to vote (some of them) for the first time. Nancy Lady Astor (1879–1964) succeeded to her husband's seat as MP for Plymouth when he became a Viscount and took her seat on the 1 December 1919. She was the second woman to be elected but the first to take her seat. She was like her husband, Waldorf, an American who settled in this country. She was a personality, rather than a serious politician, but attracted a great deal of attention in the former role. Her major success was to get a Bill through the Commons to prevent the sale of alcohol to people under 18. There is indeed an account of her participation at a meeting where she cried 'I would rather commit adultery than let liquor pass my lips.' She received a response from the back of the hall 'So would I'. She was both a witty conversationalist and the subject of wit. One conversation is recorded as her saying to Winston Churchill 'If I were your wife I would put poison in your coffee', and him replying 'And if I were your husband I would drink it.'

Margot Asquith

Margot Asquith collected caricatures of herself. She said of herself that she had no face, only two profiles. It is doubtful if she would include this in her collection.

Profile

Margot Asquith, Countess of Oxford (1864–1945) was the second wife of Herbert Henry Asquith, later Earl of Oxford. She was very much dedicated first to encouraging his political career, and then defending his reputation during and after his period as Prime Minister. A woman of intellect, she liked engaging with, particularly, men with the same qualities. While her wealth helped her husband in sustaining his political career, her tactlessness and scathing comments on other people made her to some extent a liability (see Kitchener). Of Lloyd George, she said that 'He could not see a belt without hitting below it.' In contrast about her husband she said that 'His modesty is so extreme as to be a deformity'. Like many women of her time she was not a feminist. In 1943 she said 'I cannot imagine a greater calamity for these islands were they to be put under the guidance of a woman in 10 Downing Street.'

Lady Violet Bonham–Carter (1887–1969)

Profile

The daughter of Asquith by his first marriage, she married his political secretary and remained involved in Liberal politics throughout her life. She adored her father, and was a resolute defender of his reputation. Although unsuccessful in several attempts to become an MP after 1945 (with Churchill's support) she was made a Peer in her own right in 1964. Like her father she was an extremely effective speaker both at public meetings and later on radio. She held various honorary appointments in the arts world for example at the Old Vic and the Glyndebourne Arts Trust.

Should She Take a Gamble for The Arts

This cartoon of Jennie Lee refers to her responsibility as Arts Minister. She is using a snooker cue to dispense coins.

Profile

The widow of Nye Bevan, Baroness Lee of Asheridge (1904–1988) had actually preceded him as a fiery Independent Labour Party MP from 1929–1935. She was again an MP this time for the official Labour Party from 1945 to 1970. Though her responsibilities embraced the arts, she is best remembered for her most significant action in creating the Open University. Here her radical views on the entitlement of people who had not wanted or who had not been successful in attending the traditional universities carried through a major reform which has continued to this day.

Megan Lloyd George (1902–1966)

Two caricatures of Megan Lloyd George by Sallon have been included showing her at different times in her life. In the first from the 1920s she is shown as the gay daughter of Lloyd George – still Miss because Lloyd George had not then taken his Peerage. She became Lady Megan Lloyd George when he took an Earldom in 1945.

She was deeply attached to her father, but antagonistic to his mistress Frances Stevenson who became his second wife and Countess Lloyd George. An MP herself from 1929 to 1951, she was a Liberal MP but essentially for many years just a Lloyd George party MP. In 1955 she left the Liberals to join the Labour Party which she said now represented her ideas more effectively, and was a Labour MP from 1957 to 1966. Like her father and indeed like Violet Bonham-Carter she was in her prime a very effective speaker. This is the last cartoon in the book showing a woman wearing a hat, as used to be obligatory.

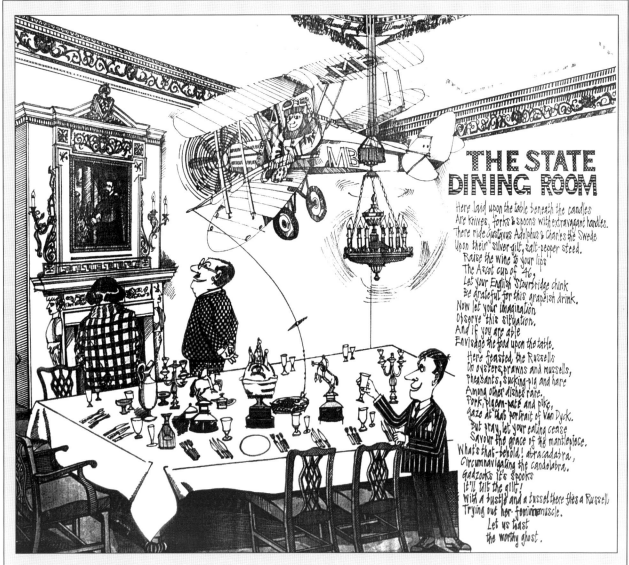

The Flying Duchess (1865–1937) – cartoonist unknown

The wife of 11th Duke of Bedford, she set up and ran medical facilities at Woburn that were used both during First World War and after it. Her fame however arises from the fact that she learnt to fly from the age of 61 – and died in a flight in 1937. She engaged in pioneer flights to India in 1928 and South Africa in 1930. The extraordinary courage of anyone learning to fly at a relatively advanced age at that time is worthy of recognition. Apart from the thrill of flying, she gained additional advantage from the fact that in the air her deafness and tinnitus were less evident.

Barbara Castle

This cartoon was published at the time of her death in 2002. The clenched fist and tight mouth are illustrations of her 'conviction politics'.

Profile

This cartoon illustrates the fact that Baroness Barbara Castle (1910–2002) had survived as an active campaigner into old age, but also her significance in the arrival of women at the top in politics. Although she was not the first woman cabinet minister, she was the first to make a really significant impact. An adherent of Nye Bevan, her red hair and impassioned speaking style led to a correct association between these physical characteristics and her politics. As a Cabinet Minister she was responsible for introducing the breathalyser to change the culture of drinking and driving – a brave act which saved lives. She was also the initiator of the Equal Pay Act. Her attempt later to reform industrial relations, through her paper 'In place of strife' was destroyed by the failure of her Cabinet colleagues to support her. Sacked by Jim Callaghan when he became Prime Minister in 1976, she continued her major involvement in politics first through the European Parliament, and then by a long campaign to make state pensions earnings related rather than inflation related. Like Margaret Thatcher she was particularly disliked by men who did not know how to deal with women.

Marcia Williams

The cartoon by Jon in the *Daily Mail* refers to the ennoblement by Harold Wilson of his political secretary Marcia Williams. Wilson is shown as small; deferring to Marcia – who was not in fact tall.

Profile

Marcia Williams, Lady Falkender (1932–) was Harold Wilson's political secretary from 1956 to his resignation in 1976. She was protective of him, yet could argue with him in a style previously unknown in relation to prime minister –political secretary relationships. There is some disagreement on the amount of influence she actually had on him. Rumours about this particularly centred on her contribution to Wilson's last honours list. Because she wrote out Wilson's final recommendations, supposedly on lavender note paper, it was claimed inaccurately that it was more her list than his.

My god! It's about time we had a woman driver!

In this cartoon from March 1979 Cummings presents a view of Margaret Thatcher as a presumably careful driver – not a prescient view of how she actually ran her Government.

'By the way I take it that you've no rooted objection to blue blood'

Maudie Littlehampton's question in this cartoon by Osbert Lancaster has just the small element of believability which makes it really funny.

Profile

Maudie Lady Littlehampton emerged in Osbert Lancaster's *Daily Express* pocket cartoons at the end of the 1940s. Although not an odd creation given Lancaster's social interests, it was paradoxical that she should appear in a middle class mass circulation newspaper. The accentuation of the sharp lips and thin legs seemed somehow particularly aristocratic. The statement she makes or the questions she raises are nearly always observations related to the supposed beliefs of the titled classes (she was married to the Earl of Littlehampton), to the way in which titled people looked at the world, and to the sustained beliefs on what was right in it.

Shirley Williams

Trog's 1981 cartoon, at the time of the evolution of the SDP shows her as neat, whereas most cartoonists portrayed her as dishevelled.

Profile

Placed side by side in 1974, there would have been no doubt as to which of Margaret Thatcher and Baroness Shirley Williams (1930–) was the more likely to become prime minister. Thatcher seized her opportunity when she threw over Ted Heath; Shirley Williams never really had the opportunity. Daughter of Vera Brittain, she was the epitome of British reasonableness, in contrast to Barbara Castle and Margaret Thatcher. Reasonableness could sometimes lead to indecision. Roy Jenkins said of her that he never came away from an encounter with her 'without being encouraged, bewitched, inspirited, yet also totally mystified about what she was going to do next.' The timbre of her voice and style of speaking exactly accompanied the content, so that she had the ability to persuade the public through radio and television.

Her disaffection with the direction of the Labour Party led her to join with Roy Jenkins, David Owen and Bill Rodgers and break the mould of British politics through setting up the Social Democratic Party. After the merger with the Liberals she continued in national politics, and became Leader of the Party in the House of Lords.

13

The House of Lords at Work

The main features of recent history in the House of Lords as a political institution have been covered in Chapter 2. Its general role as a revising chamber, and the justification for its role and powers are not easily portrayed in cartoons. However the specific activities of the House of Lords in relation to particular bills or issues of the moment do appear.

It has been claimed, most often by members of the House of the Lords themselves, that it provides a much better quality of debate than the Commons. It has sometimes delayed or improved legislation – but has allowed some, particularly originating from a Conservative Government, to go through relatively unscathed. The slightly self-congratulatory tone offered about themselves by some Peers is caught in one or two of the cartoons here.

It is the nature of the political cartoonists that they criticise rather than celebrate. Inevitably, the cartoons in this chapter represent an unbalanced satirical view of the Lords at work.

A gift from the Greeks

Tenniel's *Punch* cartoon in 1892, implies that the Irish Local Government Bill is not only a Tory horse but a Trojan horse as well. It is an interesting reflection on the times that references to classical literature of this kind could be made and understood.

PUNCH, OR THE LONDON CHARIVARI.—February 27, 1892.

A GIFT FROM THE GREEKS.

Right Hon. Arthur. "IF I CAN ONLY GET THIS THROUGH, IT OUGHT TO SETTLE 'EM!"

'Bill' the Giant Killer

In this *Punch* cartoon Tenniel refers to the attempt to reform the voting system – 'the franchise' – in 1884. Bill, oddly attired with sword, plumes and a peculiar looking horn is standing at the gate of the House of Lords, over which the Marquess of Salisbury, his principal opponent, looms.

Profile

The 3rd Marquess of Salisbury (1830–1903) at this time was the leader of the Conservative opposition to the then Liberal Government. He was the first descendant from the Cecils who had served Elizabeth to make a significant political contribution. He served as Secretary of State for India before later becoming Foreign Secretary. He was three times Prime Minister and a believer in rockhard traditional Conservative views. He ended the career of Randolph Churchill, the Tory democrat. It is a feature of a different age that he was both Prime Minister while in the House of Lords (the last), and combined being Foreign Secretary and Prime Minister.

The backwoodsman

Vicky in his cartoon of the 31 May 1956 portrays one major feature of the long post second war battle over the abolition of the death penalty. Abolition Bills from the House of Commons were rejected by the House of Lords. The two opponents here are Sidney Silverman, the Labour originator of the Bill, and the Conservative 5th Marquess of Salisbury.

Profile

Known as Bobbety as an MP, 5th Marquess of Salisbury (1893–1972) had resigned from a junior Foreign Office post with Eden in 1938. He became Leader of the Lords in 1942. He fought the reduction of the delaying power of the Lords from two years to one year, but formulated what was called the 'Salisbury doctrine'. This said that peers would not impede legislation that had been included in a government's manifesto. A senior minister under Eden, he resigned later from Macmillan's Government. He produced a memorable political comment about Iain Macleod for being 'too clever by half'.

HAVING PASSED THE COMMITTEE STAGE IN THE COMMONS, MR. SILVERMAN'S BILL TO ABOLISH HANGING WILL COME UP FOR THE THIRD READING, AFTER WHICH IT GOES TO THE LORDS.

THE BACKWOODSMEN

END DEATH PENALTY BILL

Vicky

Profile

Sidney Silverman (1898–1968) was a leftwing Labour MP, and critic of his own party, he took through the abolition of the death penalty in a Private Member's Bill but with government support, in 1965.

'We'll never know which way he would have voted on euthanasia'

In this *Times* cartoon in 1969 Richard Willson suggests that a dead peer could still be in his seat. This is not in fact wholly far fetched, because neither MPs nor Lords are allowed officially to die in their Chambers. It is tempting to see the peer on the right as Harold Macmillan but the cartoon predates his Earldom.

The Lords' Image

In 1981 the House of Lords agreed to let in a few artists and photographers to record their Lordships at work. In this drawing for *Punch*, John Jensen produced his version of how Francis Bacon might have drawn them. Included in the drawing are Lords Carrington, Hailsham, RA Butler and Longford. (See Chapters 6 and 15 for profiles on them.)

New suits

Marc suggests (*Guardian* 29 November 1984) one reaction to a decision by the House of Lords to allow in television cameras. Uncharacteristically the Lords was ahead of the Commons in its decision.

'It's gratifying how many members of the aristocracy have ordered new suits'

War Crimes Bill

In this cartoon in 1991 Garland shows that the War Crimes Bill was passed, through the operation of the Parliament Act, despite votes in the House of Lords. Garland is a great user of metaphorical and referential cartoons. The Commons as a lion and the Lords as a unicorn is not an analogy readily understood in the twenty-first century.

'Good shot my lord'

The House of Lords in what was said to be the most dramatic show of defiance in living memory voted down the Government's proposed voting system for European elections. Garland in the *Daily Telegraph* 19 November 1988 shows hunters who have killed a tiger cub. Tony Blair as the tiger is drawn to imply that this fifth defeat to the bill will encourage him to undertake reform of the House of Lords.

"GOOD SHOT, MY LORD!"

Lords back dope

As is usually the case with cartoonists, Dave Brown for the *Independent* (12 November 1996) draws peers in their robes although they rarely appear in these except at the formal opening of Parliament or Coronations. The Lords had taken an unusually permissive stance about the possibility of marijuana being used with people who were terminally ill. The grim reaper however implies that the hereditary peers are themselves terminal cases and therefore need the support of dope.

'If the good Lord had intended us . . .'

Steve Bell for the *Guardian* on 2 February 2000 gives a characteristically violent view of debates in the House of Lords which centred on homosexuality. The figure on the left is no doubt Long Longford, and the woman peer in the middle is Baroness Young who led the fight against any adjustment in the law, particularly relating to Clause 28 which prohibited the teaching about homosexuality in schools. The exclamation 'content' relates to the fact that votes in the House of Lords are expressed as content or not content – in the Commons ayes and noes have it.

Profile

Made a peer in 1971, Janet Lady Young (1926–2002) was the Leader of the House of Lords from 1981–83. She held other government posts up to 1987. Her opposition to what those in favour called tolerance in the law about homosexuality, and particularly any reduction in the age of consent, gave her prominence in her later years. Her efforts were recognised by distinction through an award 'Parliamentarian of the Year' in 2000, and 'Peer of the Year in 2001'.

'Fancy a quick 'no' job'

Not all cartoons progress beyond an original sketch, or in final form into publication. Rowson's cartoon was not published. It shows two peers (in every sense) in the physical environment which gays were characterised as operating in. This was particularly the case for Bradwell, previously Tom Driberg – thus the writing on the wall – 'Lord Bracknell was ere'.

Ten Lords a Leaping

Debates on the abolition of fox hunting are as frequent as those on the abolition of the death penalty for humans used to be. The Lords Leaping in Clive Duggan's cartoon for the *Times* of 4 January 2003 are representative rather than actual Lords.

14

Reform of the House of Lords – Continued

We left the issues about the reform of the House of Lords after the great convulsion which led to the Parliament Act of 1912, which set considerable limits on the ability of the House of Lords to revise or reject legislation passed up from the Commons. Although discussion about the powers of the Lords continued in a desultory fashion, no major change was introduced until 1948. Attlee's Labour Government tried an all party conference to decide on what should be done, but in the absence of any agreement proceeded to reduce the delaying power of the Lords to one year.

The next significant step was taken by Harold Macmillan's Conservative Government in 1958, when Life Peerages were introduced. These had originally been proposed by his Conservative predecessor in 1888 which shows as with every other aspect of the House of Lords that no intemperate haste was involved. However another major change was introduced relatively soon after this, as the right of an hereditary Peer to 'disclaim' his Peerage was made law in 1963. As described below, the ability to disclaim was brought about by the obduracy of the 2nd Lord Stansgate, some time Anthony Neil Wedgwood Benn, later Tony Benn. Members of the Labour Party may wonder whether the survival therefore of Tony Benn as a major politician was wholly beneficial; it had other consequences which Labour people might well see as advantageous. The 14th Earl of Home, who had originally opposed the right to disclaim, showed unexpected ambition in

'Maudie darling please . . .'

The Earl of Littlehampton himself appears with Maudie Littlehampton in this cartoon for the *Daily Express*. It is a reference to the initiative by Harold Macmillan's Government to introduce life peerages. The details of Maudie's undressed state may be unfamiliar to younger readers.

"Maudie, darling, *please*—just for today could we call a truce to all further speculation about the identity of the first life peeresses?"

1963 and became Sir Alec Douglas-Home and Prime Minister but lost the subsequent election to the commoner Harold Wilson.

The Labour Party, which in principle wanted to abolish the House of Lords but could not agree on a possible replacement, had argued against Life Peers because they would help to sustain an improper institution. However it moved pragmatically to take advantage of the opportunities to reward followers, and sometimes recognised the necessity to appoint participants in the continuing business conducted in the Lords.

The Labour Government's Reform Bill in 1967 was defeated, in large part through the extraordinary combination of Enoch Powell and Michael Foot.

Tony Blair's Labour Government of 1997 decided to grapple with the easiest part of the issue, which was to abolish the hereditary component. Discussions and manoeuvres over this resulted variously in the removal of the then Labour Leader of the House of Lords (Ivor Richard), and the later removal of the Conservative Leader (Cranborne). The eventual 'Stage 1' compromise led to an even more bizarre British phenomenon than usual, the election by hereditary Peers of ninety of their own number to remain in the House. At the time of writing the further reform of the House of Lords – or a renamed Second Chamber was in limbo. The Commons voted against all seven options in February 2003.

'What does the fella think he is – a socialist?'

Herbert Morrison and Clement Attlee, now both peers, in Vicky's cartoon 25 November 1960 associate the renunciation of a peerage with socialism. Paradoxically at that time Benn was not a leftwing socialist.

Herbert Morrison – Lord Morrison of Lambeth (1888–1965)

Morrison had what was then normal background for a Labour politician. He was born into a working class family, was a shop assistant before becoming involved in a trade union. His prime political experience initially was on the London County Council which he led. He was also an MP, and as Minister of Transport in the Labour Government of 1929 to 1931 would have been candidate to become leader of the Parliamentary Party if he

"WHAT DOES THE FELLER THINK HE IS – A SOCIALIST?"

had been re-elected to Parliament in 1931. Attlee was already Leader however when he returned in 1935. He was Home Secretary in Churchill's wartime Cabinet. He was a major contributor as an organiser for Labour's historic victory in 1945. His version of public ownership – nationalisation – was carried through by the Labour Government 1945–1951. He had tried unsuccessfully to supplant Attlee in 1945. His feel for British politics was of no help to him when Attlee made him Foreign Secretary. He was an exemplar of some of the best, and worst features, of the traditional Labour Party. His belief that effort and skill rather than birth should be rewarded was based on more than his own achievements.

Tony Benn (1925–)

Elected as an MP in 1950, he tried to renounce the title to which he succeeded in 1960. He was disqualified from the Commons, won the subsequent by election, was again disqualified but eventually succeeded in getting enough support to allow renunciation. Of his many campaigns this was Benn's most successful. He brought about the referendum on Britain's membership of the European Community, pressed his ideas on socialist policies and democratisation within the Labour Party and was only defeated by a tiny vote for the Deputy Leadership in 1981. This was the high point of his career, in terms of acquiring power in Parliament. The cartoon in this chapter represents him very mildly. Subsequently he was demonised especially by rightwing cartoonists such as Cummings.

'That's no membership card – beat it'

Tony Benn had been forced out of the House of Commons following his succession to the title Lord Stansgate. In a by election he stood and secured the majority shown on the paper he is holding. However R A Butler Leader of the House of Commons is shown telling him to go away in a cartoon by Papas on 8 May 1961 for the *Guardian*.

R A Butler (1902–1982)

No other politician has got as close as Butler twice did to becoming prime minister, but not succeeding. Despite his pre war career as a proponent of appeasement Churchill made him Secretary of State for Education in his wartime Cabinet. Butler produced in 1944 the Education Act which led to the transformation of opportunities offered to a much larger number of young people through secondary education after the war. He was a Tory reformer, and helped to create the more liberal Toryism accepted by Churchill which led to the return of the Conservative Party in 1951. He was believed to be a successful Chancellor of the Exchequer from 1951–1953 – and indeed took charge of the government when Churchill and Eden were ill in 1953.

Successive appointments thereafter caused him more trouble than they secured applause. He was perhaps the first Conservative Home Secretary to have trouble with his own party because of his relative liberalism. He lost out when Macmillan succeeded Eden in 1957, and refused to fight hard enough to gain the succession to Macmillan in 1963. Political correspondents delighted in his company because he was open to the point of foolishness about policies and his colleagues. He responded to a question 'Would you say that this (Anthony Eden) is the best Prime Minister we have?' with a simple answer 'yes.' Journalists turned it into a statement by Butler, with its implication that there could be a better prime minister. Such a statement fitted the common understanding of his feline qualities.

Dressing shed

In a style quite different from that shown in his other cartoons in his book, Jensen in the *Sunday Telegraph* 1 August 1963 shows an exhilarated Benn having left his peer's robes behind. Amongst other things the cartoon captures the then view of Benn as someone with a rather pleasant expression of boyish enthusiasm – not the characteristics caught in many later cartoons.

'Redundant and not a single word about retraining'

Prior to the Blair Government's efforts from 1997, the only significant attempt to reform the House of Lords occurred in 1967, when this cartoon by Garland appeared in the *Daily Telegraph*. Redundancy and retraining were a familiar part of industrial life at this time. It was interesting to see a faint echo of this when some peers in 2002 threatened to bring a case that their employment rights were being destroyed if they were removed from the Lords.

The first reluctant peer disclaims his title

Benn was of course the first peer to take advantage of the act which enabled him to disclaim his title. In this cartoon by Vicky 21 August 1963 the representation of Benn's eyes foreshadow the exaggeration which was later given to them, to make him look fanatical. The mournful character on the beach is Lord Hailsham – who did indeed disclaim his title also.

Profile

Quintin Hogg, Viscount Hailsham, later Lord Hailsham (1907–2001) won a famous by election in Oxford in 1938, and was an MP until he succeeded his father the 1st Viscount Hailsham in 1950. He was a reluctant member of the Lords. He had cabinet posts under both Eden and Macmillan, but acquired his public reputation largely by his extravagant and extrovert performance as Chairman of the Conservative Party leading up to the 1959 victory. Initially favoured by Macmillan to succeed him in 1963, he took advantage of the ability to renounce his peerage in order to fight the leadership. He failed in that, but returned as an MP. In 1970 he reappeared as a Life Peer and Lord Chancellor first under Ted Heath and then Margaret Thatcher. He was an occasionally excitable politician in public who gave cartoonists plenty of scope. He made an explosive appearance on television at the time of the Profumo affair in 1963 'A great party is not to be brought down because of a squalid affair between a woman of easy virtue and a proved liar.' However accurate, the last phrase was seen as an uneasy fit with his deeply held Christian beliefs.

'The numbers have to be controlled'

Although the cartoons in the previous chapter might suggest otherwise, the Lords has never been wholly obsessed with issues about homosexuality. Deer hunting and fox hunting have similarly been the focus of their opposition to proposals made in the House of Commons, as Matt (Pritchett) comments in the *Daily Telegraph* of 5 December 1998.

'Their numbers have to be controlled and this is the most humane way'

In this *Guardian* cartoon of 15 October 1998 Steve Bell adversely comments on the origins and characteristics of their Lordships – and of Baroness Thatcher. It may be inaccurate, or alternatively unkind, to suggest that the Lords' spiritual was George Carey Archbishop of Canterbury.

"... only a thorough purge will guarantee a smoother running Commons".

'Only a thorough purge'

Richard Willson's *Times* cartoon of 26 November 1998 shows Margaret Jay as Leader of the Lords offering unpleasant medicine to Lord Cranborne Conservative Leader of the House of Lords. Although it is given in quotation marks it is unlikely that Margaret Jay actually delivered the pun.

Profile

Although heir to the 6th Marquess of Salisbury, Viscount Cranborne (1946–) arrived in the House of Lords in 1987 through one of the peculiar by ways leading to entry into the Lords. As Leader of the House of Lords when Tony Blair's Government showed that it was determined to abolish the hereditary peers, he decided to negotiate the best solution he could which provided for the retention of at least some hereditaries. The negotiation was successful. It was initially disowned by William Hague the Conservative Leader, who sacked him. Cranborne proclaimed his understanding that Hague was quite right to sack him. The negotiated agreement was in fact implemented.

'I don't remember him last time'

Peter Brookes in his cartoon for the *Times* of 25 November 1998 makes vivid the metaphor of the hereditary peers being 'axed' in the reformed House of Lords. The two leading peers are shown carrying the Cap of Maintenance, and the Sword of Honour at the Opening of Parliament.

"I DON'T REMEMBER HIM **LAST** TIME..."

Prize turkey

Peter Brookes on Friday in the *Times* provides a cartoon based on animals or vegetables. In this case he is able to use the familiar expression of 'turkeys voting for Christmas' in relation to the acceptance by the peers of a Reform Bill largely abolishing hereditary membership.

What do you call a chamber chosen by birth, lottery or Tony

Dave Brown in the *Independent* of 21 January 1999 shows Tony Blair wheeling Margaret Jay and an unspecific 'People's Peer' into a House of Lords in which only a drunken peer is present. The People's Peerage was intended to create opportunities for people who would not normally be considered as Life Peers. It contained echoes of Blair's description of Princess Diana as 'The People's Princess'. The actual appointees however seemed no different from those installed by existing processes.

Tony Blair (1953–)

It is perhaps remarkable that Tony Blair (1953–) has not yet described himself 'the People's Prime Minister'. He abbreviated his Christian name as a part of the process of making himself look less privileged in his background than he actually was. An MP with required leftwing views in 1983, by the time he stood for the Leadership in 1994 he represented the modernising trend in the Labour Party. By that time the Labour Party had become prepared to ditch nearly all the rhetoric and most of the reality of its previous beliefs and become electable. The massive majorities secured in 1997 and 2001, arose in large part because of his leadership, the policies he espoused and those he disdained. A benign economic environment unlike any experienced by any previous Labour Government was a massive help in producing low inflation and low unemployment. The success or failure of his other policies for example on the NHS or transport are matters of greater contention. On the House of Lords, it has become clear that his real interest was in having a House which would be no significant block to his policies. It is an entirely predictable view for anyone who is actually holding power.

(William Tell)

In yet another of his metaphorical cartoons Garland's cartoon for the *Daily Telegraph* of 22 January 1999 shows Tony Blair firing an alarmingly large arrow at the apple representing the hereditary peers. The implication presumably is that he is quite likely to knock off the head of the unfortunate peer supporting the apple.

Lord Wakeham's recommendations

After largely abolishing the hereditary element, Tony Blair set up a Royal Commission chaired by the Conservative Peer Lord Wakeham to make recommendations on how to carry through the reforms. Royal Commissions have historically been excellent at deliberating for a long time, producing solutions which can then be ignored. This was largely the case with Lord Wakeham's report, although some aspects of it including the view that appointment rather than election was likely to be the best method of creating peers eventually became Blair's chosen solution.

Profile

The daughter of Jim Callaghan, Margaret Jay (1939–) married Peter Jay the economist and television journalist. His appointment by his father-in-law to the Ambassadorship in Washington did not lead to a happy marriage – a version of some aspects of it appeared in a book and later film. She worked in television, and then returned to politics, and was given a middle level appointment by Tony Blair. In 1998 Blair removed Ivor Richard as Leader of the Lords, and appointed Margaret Jay in his place. She successfully carried through the reform which led to the removal of all but ninety hereditary peers.

'You're meek and pliable'

Matt (Pritchett) in the *Daily Telegraph* comments on the perception, pushed very hard by the Conservative Party, that Blair's appointment of Life Peers was of people who were sympathetic to his policies. Given the history of Life Peerages this does not seem an extraordinary accusation in relation to the practice of other prime ministers.

'You're meek and pliable, why aren't you a peer?'

'I am a billionaire from Belize'

Chris Riddell in the *Observer* on 2 April 2000 refers to Lord Ashcroft who donated large sums of money to the Conservative Party under William Hague, but whose formal residence was not in this country, and who apparently made a lot of money from companies he operated in Belize. The billionaire is also shown as a fat cat – a term of opprobrium to describe directors of companies who did extravagantly well out of them. The poodle however represents other appointments made by Tony Blair.

15

Stately Homes

In the 1880s as peerages were given to new types of people, not primarily landed, at much the same time some historic stately homes began to disappear. It is not clear that any legal or other distinction between country houses and stately homes has ever been agreed. Clearly you can have a quite small country house – a stately home is distinguished in part by size, perhaps more by the likelihood that it is in the possession of a member of the aristocracy. Convenience and economic necessity were usually the cause of the destruction of stately homes, both in London and in the country. As we will see in the next chapter desperate attempts to save them initially consisted of marriages between Peers or sons of Peers and heiresses from the United States of America. Indeed some new stately homes were built again by successful business people as an indication of conspicuous consumption and a claim for social status.

'Now I want you to promise me you are all going to be good evacuees and not worry his Lordship'

Since this cartoon by Giles is dated 30 July 1944 it seems to have occurred long after the first evacuees arrived in stately homes. It would have to have been related to the second wave of Nazi airborne attacks, with the V1 and V2 rockets. As always with Giles the faces of the people drawn in the cartoons are fascinating.

Stately homes both new and old were adapted for other uses – hospitals in World War I, schools before and after World War II, sometimes mysterious uses during World War II.

It has always been possible for some people to visit stately homes not just as guests but as individuals interested in the house and the possessions contained within it. For a minority this was part of a cultured education. After the Second World War two rather significantly different actions made stately homes available to a much wider public. The first was the increasing use of the National Trust. This took over effective ownership of properties either by direct purchase or by the Government accepting the house in lieu of death duties. In some cases the owners remained in situ, but the house had to be open to the public for at least a significant part of the year.

It is the second action, the opening of two stately homes and associated activities in the grounds to the general public which is mainly memorialised in the following cartoons.

Longleat, House of the 6th Marquess of Bath opened as a major attraction in 1949, and in 1966 he added Europe's first Safari Park. The 13th Duke of Bedford was the first ducal showman. He opened Woburn to the public in 1955, and followed by giving space to a nudist colony and then a Safari Park in 1970.

'Before I could say Grace he'd eaten him'

This cartoon by Emwood in the *Daily Mail* on 5 April 1966 is a humorous view of the consequence of opening by the 6th Marquess of Bath of a safari park at Longleat – the first in Europe. Lions of course were unknown outside zoos in the United Kingdom, and at this time not many people would have had experience of travelling on safari expeditions in Africa.

'Hm! No mention of what you charged for exhibiting sliding doors and secret passages or perhaps you haven't got any m'lord'

In this cartoon by Joseph Lee for the *Evening News* in May 1949 a tax inspector (see his hat and umbrella) is reviewing the opening of a stately home.

"Hm! No mention of what you charged for exhibiting sliding doors and secret passages or perhaps you havent got any, eh, M'Lord"

Anything Bath can Do

Giles' cartoon of 7 April 1966 shows the Duke of Bedford starting the process which led to the opening of his own safari park in 1970.

Profile

The 13th Duke of Bedford (1917–2002) had an upbringing which was peculiar even by the standards of the aristocracy. As a youth he was separated from his parents (though given their relationship this may not have been a bad thing), and did not know that he was the heir to the 11th Duke of Bedford, nor that the flying Duchess of Bedford was his grandmother. On his succession he decided to open Woburn Abbey to the public. He unashamedly put himself in the public eye as a way of publicising the availability of Woburn. He said that 'I've been accused of being undignified. I am. If you take your dignity to a pawn broker, he won't give you much for it.' Arguments with the trustees led to him handing the management of Woburn over abruptly to his eldest son the Marquess of Tavistock in 1974.

'It's your fault m'lord they're jealous of your new page three girl!'

The Marquesses of Bath had found Longleat, like all stately homes, immensely expensive to run. The 6th opened the first stately home to be aimed at attracting the general public in April 1949. His son had an unusual life style. This included 74 'wifelets'; his marital and non marital relationships were therefore the subject of ribald gossip. The page three girl was Sheree Gillam his 54th wifelet. The cartoon by Franklin of 9 January 1993 relates to his latest relationship. Alexander Thyn, before becoming Marquess, designed west wing murals and a Kama Sutra bedroom, undoubtedly extraordinary features of a stately home.

'If the little wretch is not claimed by closing time leave him in the Wildlife Safari Park'

The 13th Duke of Bedford opened Woburn Abbey to the public in April 1955. His intention was to make it enjoyable, and he subsequently opened both a nudist colony and later a safari park. His safari park was opened in fact by the then Marquess of Bath in 1970 – an interesting example of aristocratic camaraderie. This cartoon was published on 3 May 1987 when the Abbey was being run by the Duke of Bedford's son the Marquess of Blandford and his wife. In this context it may be that the two are an unflattering representation of the Marquess and Marchioness.

'I signed their guide book, showed them the room where I was born, told them a doubtful story about the fifth earl and what do I get – sixpence!'

This undated cartoon by Osbert Lancaster in the 1950s has a special interest. In his autobiography published in 1959, the Duke of Bedford told the story of his wife who was actually given a tip by visitors she was guiding round Woburn.

'I am sorry m'lady but I'm afraid his Grace is away on safari – right down the other end of the drive' 21X70

Maudie Littlehampton appears again, this time in reference to the creation by the Marquess of Bath of a safari park including lions at Longleat. It is not clear why Osbert Lancaster has also drawn what are apparently vultures flying overhead, except that they notoriously look for the remains left by lions.

16

These Also Served

In the 1880s peerages began to be given to people of distinction without wealth. Given his omnivorous reading habits, it is not so surprising that Gladstone was the first to give a Peerage to an author – Tennyson in 1883. Salisbury presented coronets to Leighton the artist, and to Lister from the medical world. Gladstone's initiative with authors has not been followed much by subsequent Prime Ministers. John Buchan became Lord Tweedsmuir, but this was to facilitate him becoming Governor General of Canada rather than necessarily a recognition of his literary gifts. Even further away from the literary merits of Lord Tennyson, the ennoblement of Jeffrey Archer we must hope had more to do with his services to the Conservative Party than to literature.

There have been other medical Peers – Lord Horder who looked after George 5th and Lord Moran who may well have contributed as much to keeping Winston Churchill alive as he claimed in his precedent breaking memoirs.

This chapter also celebrates the issue of American heiresses providing the funds necessary to sustain a decent (or indeed indecent) life as a peer. Other cartoons provide recognition of unusual lordly matters not covered elsewhere.

'Glad, my Lord, you have been tempted to change your hat!'

Sambourne's cartoon is a welcome given by Mr Punch to the acceptance of a peerage by the poet Alfred Tennyson. (*Punch* 22 December 1883)

Profile

Alfred Lord Tennyson (1809–1892). He was a hugely popular poet, at a time when this had much more significance than it would do in the 20th and 21st centuries. Indeed he was in his earlier days rather more a popular than a critical success. His major poems included *In memoriam, Charge of the Light Brigade.* It would during his lifetime have been the sign of a decent middle class intelligence to be able to be quote extensively from his poems. He was buried in Westminster Abbey.

'So much for the provinces – when do we open in the West End?'

In this cartoon by Trog, the Earl of Snowdon and the Duke of Norfolk are shown in their dual role in managing the investiture of the Prince of Wales at Caernarvon Castle in 1969. This was 'modern' in that the set and costumes were designed by the Earl of Snowdon, the Prince of Wales' brother in law.

Profile

Marmaduke Fitzallan Howard, 16th Duke of Norfolk (1908–1975), was the hereditary Earl Marshall of England. As such he was responsible for grand national events such as the funeral of George V, the Coronations of George VI and Elizabeth II, and most noticeably of all the funeral of Winston Churchill. Norfolk was a lifelong devotee of the turf and the manager of the MCC tour to Australia from 1962–1963 (although the more practical aspects were run by Alec Bedser). He had a new cricket ground built at his home Arundel Castle and in the early days played in it himself. This produced one of the more interesting umpiring stories. His butler was an umpire when the Duke batted but failed to make his ground when running. On appeal the umpire's decision was 'your Grace is not in'.

Silencing Lord Winston

This cartoon by Paul Slater in *The Week* 22 January 2000 refers to the fact that Lord Winston a Labour sympathising peer had criticised the effectiveness of the NHS. He is about to be injected by Alastair Campbell the Government's main spin-doctor.

Profile

Robert, Lord Winston (1940–) became famous through his work on human fertility – he was Professor of Fertility Studies from 1987 onwards. In this field his research gave hope and the actuality of birth to women previously lacking either. He became a significant contributor on television, broadening beyond his original specialism.

'Strictly between Earls, Littlehampton, I don't mind admittin' that it's not having to clock in which hurts, but bein' on a flat rate with all those viscounts and barons.'
10VIII1957

In this 1957 cartoon Osbert Lancaster is referring to the decision to get Lords to sign in on the days on which they were claiming expenses for attending the House. The bowler hatted figure of the Earl of Littlehampton is accompanied by a representation of a more backwoodsman type peer. His eccentricity seems to be displayed in what looked like spats on his feet, which seem an unlikely accompaniment to a hairy tweed suit.

The fair bride and her puny husband

In the American magazine *Life*, the social cartoonist Charles Dana Gibson is referring to the marriage between Consuela Vanderbilt and the Duke of Marlborough on 6 November 1895. She was one of the earliest of the American heiresses whose financial support enabled the British aristocracy to survive in a style close to that which they regarded as right. She brought $15 million at those days values. It was not a happy marriage. In 1920 Consuela was allowed an annulment by the Catholic Church because the marriage had been entered into under duress.

A new international interest

The American gold fields for impecunious British noblemen is the subtitle for this cartoon (22 September 1880) in *Puck* by Opper. Sweet faced American heiresses are offering their dollars – or probably their fathers' dollars – to much less attractive peers who are however giving them marriage.

Cheer up girls

This cartoon (7 November 1895) in the American magazine *Life* refers to the belief that more American heiresses are available for more peers.

Love at first sight (*Puck* 6 November 1895)

The cartoon is explicit about what the peer is interested in; while the American woman adopts a romantic pose, the peer has his hands stretched out not towards her but to the dollar-laden packages.

Gerald 6th Duke of Westminster (1951 to date)

Marc's cartoon seems rather unfair – in portraying the Duke with a rather supercilious air. He has not been involved in politics but has a large range of charitable interests through which he does good work for less well provided people.

Profile

It has long since ceased to be a requirement that Lords should have massive areas of land to support or justify their peerage. In a sense the Duke of Westminster with his vast property interests is a throwback. He is included here however as an example of the way in which some members of the peerage have managed to continue a family line without it being ruined financially despite some quite extravagant predecessors. He is usually quoted high up in the list of the richest people in the UK.

17

Scandals

There are of course people who regard the continued existence of an hereditary Peerage as scandalous – and rather fewer who see even Life Peerages to be offensive to egalitarian principles. The supporters of hereditary and Life Peerages have sometimes found the expression of their views more difficult, or at least their sense more challenged, by occasional scandals involving Peers. The following collection is of course not at all representative of the general behaviour of Peers. It is not even particularly representative of the scandals that have occurred. It is interesting to find that some scandals that appeared in print did not attract the attention of cartoonists in a perhaps less prurient time, see for example the Ampthill paternity case in 1921, and the Duchess of Argyll divorce case in 1963.

The issue of the extent to which public interest in the (literally) affairs of individuals in the public eye seems to have been in effect largely resolved in favour of publishing anything about such an individual. The 'public interest' has been defined as 'the interest of the public'. As far as cartoonists are concerned there may have been less willingness to draw about anyone other than politicians in terms of scandals.

Discipline a la Kenyon

In this Gillray cartoon of 25 March 1797, the Lord Chief Justice Kenyon is depicted as flogging Lady Buckingham. She (and more peeresses are shown in the stocks at the top of the cartoon) had indulged in the gambling game faro. Kenyon had wanted to punish 'any persons found guilty of gaming offences, whatever may be their rank and station in the country.' This punishment was not actually carried out.

Discipline à la Kenyon.

Lord Queensberry (1844–1900)

In this caricature (© estate of Max Beerbohm) Max Beerbohm shows the 8th Marquess of Queensberry. Although Queensberry had produced the rules which turned boxing from a wholly brutal activity into a better managed process, his notoriety rather than fame occurred in relation to his son. Lord Alfred Douglas was involved in a homosexual relationship with Oscar Wilde. Wilde made the mistake of responding through the Law Courts to Queensberry's accusations. As a result Wilde was convicted of homosexual activities, sent to jail and died in penury in Paris.

I could not love thee

Bernard Partridge's *Punch* cartoon of 26 July 1926 shows that the scandal of the purchase of political honours still existed despite the fact that a committee had been set up after 1922 to monitor the award honours including peerages.

Treasure Island

In this cartoon 3 December 1927 Low is commenting on the Lloyd George fund. This had been largely derived from the sale of honours. Three of the four dancers – Viscount Reading, Earl Beauchamp and Sir Herbert Samuel were Liberal leaders. Low has included himself, for no obvious reason. A different scandal occurred later in relation to Beauchamp.

"TREASURE ISLAND".

Profile

Earl Beauchamp (1872–1938). He was the Leader of the Liberal Party in the House of Lords from 1924–1931. The *Dictionary of National Biography* says he suddenly resigned in 1931 and went to live abroad, but with delicacy did not reveal the reasons. He was about to be prosecuted for homosexuality. The case had echoes of Oscar Wilde, since Beauchamp had initiated a legal case against his brother in law 'Bendor' Duke of Westminster, who spread accusations about him. King George V is reported as saying 'I thought men like that shot themselves.' The scandal is worth noting because of what it says about 1931 – and about the different laws and standards of the 21st Century.

'So I says to my mate . . . '

The connection between the award of honours and contributions to party political funds continues to the present day. (See Riddell's cartoon in Chapter 15). In this case Mac's *Daily Mail* cartoon on 7 September 1999 is commenting on the revelation that a number of wealthy businessmen had been ennobled after giving funds to the Labour Party. The idea that a meths drinking lottery winner could become a peer is a different kind of cartoonists' exaggeration.

"... So I says to my mate, Shamus back at the mission, what am I goin' to do with me lottery win? Why not make a donation to the Labour Party he says ..."

The Getaway Man

Emwood on 4 June 1973 shows Lord Lambton (who often wore dark glasses in public), pursued by the press. Lambton disclaimed his Peerage in 1970 when he would have become the 6th Earl of Durham but retained his courtesy title. He was set up and photographed in bed with two women. It is not clear why Emwood drew one dog eating another.

'It is fortunate I have not been stripped of my peerage'

This shows Lord Kagan on 8 May 1980 in the *Daily Express*. Kagan had been ennobled by Harold Wilson, who is shown wearing the Gannex raincoat through which Kagan had acquired fame. He served ten months in prison for theft and false accounting though in his defence it was said he used money to help refugees from behind the Iron Curtain.

Toppled people?

Trog's cartoon of 16 October 1983 shows the departure of Cecil Parkinson. He had conducted an affair with, and produced a daughter by Sarah Keyes, which led to his resignation.

Profile

Cecil Parkinson's (1931–) move up the ministerial ladder under Margaret Thatcher culminated in his appointment as Party Chairman, and the success he managed on her behalf in 1983 election. He might well have been appointed Foreign Secretary except for this scandal. His career as a minister was restored later but in a lower level of ministerial appointment than he might otherwise have had. Memories of the scandal were frequently revived because Sarah Keyes fought very hard for what she saw as the rights of her daughter.

In addition to the wifelets referred to in Chapter 16, the then Marquess of Bristol was accused of indulging in other stimuli. Jak's *Evening Standard* cartoon of 1 August 1986 provides an improbable scenario.

'I fear gentlemen, to use one of your expressions, the Marquess has lammed it'

Mac on 20 October 1999 in the *Daily Mail* suggests a rather odd celebration of the official declaration of the death of the 7th Earl of Lucan. Lucan disappeared in November 1974 immediately after the killing in his Belgravia home of the family nanny, and the attempted murder of his wife. Questions about how he had disappeared, and whether he was still alive created a number of different theories – and a large number of 'sightings'. He was a heavy gambler and was estranged from his wife.

'By jove! We've got something to celebrate today, Lucan old chap. You've been declared officially dead'

Dave Gaskill in *Today* uses the stately home environment to comment on Jamie Marquess of Blandford in 1992. He had been sentenced to jail for not paying maintenance to his wife, but was released after only three days.

'. . . And over the centuries the dukes have progressively adopted a more simple form of attire'

The Ballad of Bellmarsh Jail

Trog shows Jeffrey Archer using his time in jail to write yet another book. His revelations were against prison rules, but he was not given further punishment.

Profile

Jeffrey, Lord Archer (1940–) of Weston Supermare's career as a successful novelist arose initially from one of his earliest problems. He wrote his first novel in order to recoup his losses on a failed business venture. Thereafter he was rarely out of the public eye either as a novelist or a politician. It was cruelly said of him that he disproved the proposition that everyone could write one bad novel. He never returned to the Commons but developed a parallel career as an active political figure. A successful fundraiser, he became Deputy Chairman of the Conservative Party but resigned over a scandal involving a prostitute. He successfully sued for libel, was made a Peer in 1992, but was found guilty of perjury in 2001. He received a four-year jail sentence. His penal punishment was extended by the Committee of the Marylebone Cricket Club, who suspended his membership for seven years.

Stand by Your Man

In his cartoon of 27 July 2001 Dave Gaskill shows Lady Mary Archer as the prime figure in front of Jeffrey Archer strumming a guitar. The judge in his original libel trial had compared the possibility of rubber insulated sex with Jeffrey Archer's marriage to Mary – 'is she not fragrant?' She continued to support him, in or out of jail.

18

Winston Spencer Churchill

Churchill is presented here because he did not become a Peer, not because he was one. In the 20th Century, after Salisbury, already a Marquess, ex Prime Ministers received an Earldom unless they were dying or dead – Campbell-Bannerman, Bonar Law, Macdonald, Chamberlain; Harold Wilson broke the convention for himself. Precisely because "ordinary" prime ministers received an Earldom, it was thought that Churchill might be offered a Dukedom. At the appropriate time, conversation ensued between his Private Secretary and that of Queen Elizabeth II. The latter reported that the Queen would not give a Dukedom to Churchill, since she would only now give such a title to a member of the Royal Family. It was not clear that Churchill in fact wanted to be a Duke. It was however agreed in a fashion which might well be unique to the British Aristocracy and Monarchy that the Queen should suggest in their final interview that a Dukedom might be available, but that Sir Winston would decline – which he did.

The long political career of Winston Churchill which led up to this non offer is surely familiar to all educated Britons – he even managed to secure a majority vote in a 2003 BBC poll for the most famous English person of all time. Thus his career from early life as an unsuccessful student at Harrow, as a soldier and journalist before becoming Conservative MP have been well set out not least in his own books. He left the Conservative Party to become in combination with Lloyd George a leader of radical Government measures aiding the poor in the Liberal Government of 1906. His career after the 1st World War fluctuated, but was generally downwards. His high point as Chancellor of the Exchequer 1924–1929 was followed by a lonely experience in opposing first any significant independence for India, and second in drawing attention to the threat posed by Hitler and Nazism in Germany. He led the country to victory in the 2nd World War, claiming with undue modesty at his eightieth birthday celebration in Westminster Hall that he only gave "The lion's roar".

He was a favoured figure of attention for cartoonists, who often drew attention to the extraordinary variety of his headgear, though latterly his cigar was ever present. The cartoon has been chosen because it illustrates him in stages until his eightieth birthday by which time he was a Knight of the Garter.

19

The Cartoonists

The publication(s) shown are those with which the cartoonist was primarily associated.

Aislin (Terry Mosher)	1943–	*Montreal Star*
APE (Carlo Pillegrini)	1839–1889	*Vanity Fair*
Max Beerbohm	1872–1956	Many publications
Steve Bell	1951–	*The Guardian*
Nicolas Bentley	1907–1978	Many publications
Timothy Birdsall	1936–1963	*Spectator, Private Eye, That Was the Week* (TV)
Peter Brookes	1943–	*The Times*
Dave Brown	1957–	*The Independent*
Leo Cheney	1878–1928	*Manchester Evening News, Daily Mail*
George Cruikshank	1792–1878	Social and Political Prints
Michael Cummings	1919–1997	*Daily* and *Sunday Express* and *Punch*
Will Dyson	1880–1938	*Daily Herald*
Emmwood (John Musgrove Wood)	1915–1999	*Daily Mail*
Clive Francis	1946–	(No newspaper association)
Stanley Franklin	1930–	*Daily Mirror* and *Sun*
Harry Furniss	1854–1925	*Punch*
Nicholas Garland	1935–	*Daily Telegraph, Independent, Spectator*
Dave Gaskill	1939–	*Today, News of the World, Sun*
Carl Giles	1916–1995	*Daily* and *Sunday Express*
James Gillray	1756–1815	Social and Political Prints
Francis Carruthers Gould	1844–1925	*Westminster Gazette, Picture Politics*
Charles Griffin	1946–	*Daily Mirror*
HB (John Doyle)	1797–1868	Political Prints
Ted Harrison	1948–	Book *"Modern Elizabethans"*
L Raven Hill	1867–1942	*Punch*
William Hogarth	1697–1764	Social and Political Prints
Jak (Raymond Jackson)	1927–1997	*Evening Standard*
John Jensen	1930–	*Punch, Sunday Telegraph, Now*
Jon (William John Philpin Jones)	1913–1992	*Daily Mail*
John Kent	1937–2003	*Guardian, Times, Private Eye*

Osbert Lancaster	1908–1986	*Daily Express*
Joseph Lee	1901–1974	*Evening News*
David Low	1891–1963	*London Evening Star, Evening Standard, Daily Herald, Guardian*
Mac (Stan McMurtry)	1936–	*Daily Mail*
Marc (Mark Boxer)	1931–1988	*Times, Sunday Times, Guardian, Observer, New Statesman*
Matt (Matthew Pritchett)	1964–	*Daily* and *Sunday Telegraph*
Matt (Matthew Sandford)	1875–1943	*Daily Sketch, Daily Graphic*
Nicola (Nicola Jennings)	1958–	*Daily Mirror, Observer, Guardian, Sunday Times, Punch*
William Papas	1927–2000	*Guardian, Sunday Times, Punch*
Bernard Partridge	1861–1945	*Punch*
Paul Pry (William Heath)	1795–1840	Political Prints
Poy (Percy Fearon)	1874–1948	*Daily Despatch, London Evening News, Daily Mail*
Chris Riddell	1962–	*Economist, Independent, Observer*
Thomas Rowlandson	1756–1827	Political Prints
Martin Rowson	1959–	*Today, Guardian, Time Out, Daily Mirror, Tribune*
Ralph Sallon	1899–1999	*Jewish Chronicle, Daily Herald, Daily Mirror*
Linley Sambourne	1844–1910	*Punch*
Gerald Scarfe	1936–	*Private Eye, Sunday Times*
Ernest Shepard	1879–1976	*Punch*
Gary (Gary Smith)	1963–	*Sunday Times, Daily Mail*
Paul Slater	1953–	*The Week, Times*
John Springs	1962–	*Independent, Financial Times*
Spy (Leslie Ward)	1851–1922	*Vanity Fair*
Sidney (George) Strube	1892–1950	*Daily Express*
John Tenniel	1820–1914	*Punch*
Bert Thomas	1883–1966	*The World, Punch*
Feliks Topolski	1907–1989	*Topolski Chronicles*
George Townshend	1724–1807	Political Prints
Trog (Wally Fawkes)	1924–	*Daily Mail, Punch, Observer, Today, Sunday Telegraph*
Vicky (Victor Weisz)	1913–1966	*News Chronicle, Evening Standard, Daily Mirror, New Statesman*
Richard Willson	1939–	*Times, Sunday Times*

Acknowledgements

The author is grateful to all the copyright holders who gave permission for cartoons to appear in this book. Unfortunately it was not possible to trace all copyright holders.

Atlantic Syndication for Associated Newspapers
 Cartoons by Jak, Emmwood, Lee, Low, Mac, Poy, Vicky
Curtis Brown Group on behalf of the Estate of Nicolas Bentley
Express Newspapers
 Cartoons by Cummings, Giles, Jak, Lancaster, Vicky
London Management for the Estate of Max Beerbohm
 Cartoons of Kitchener, Queensberry
Mirror Group Newspapers
 Cartoon by Vicky
News International
 Cartoon by Brookes, Duggan, Kent, Willson
Punch Cartoon Library
 Cartoons by Bentley, Jensen, Partridge, Raven Hill, Shepard
Sun Newspapers
 Cartoons by Franklin
Telegraph Newspapers
 Cartoons by Garland, Matt
Trustees for Children of Mark Boxer
 Cartoons by Marc

Steve Bell
Adam Birdsall (for Timothy)
Dave Brown
Daniel Fearon (for Poy)
Wally Fawkes (Trog)
Anna Ford (for Mark Boxer)
Clive Francis
David Gaskill
Charles Griffin
Ted Harrison
Nicola Jennings
John Jensen

Tessa Papas (for Papas)
Sylvia Philpin Jones (for Jon)
Chris Riddell
Martin Rowson
Philip Sallon (for Sallon)
Gerald Scarfe
Paul Slater
Gary Smith (Gary)
John Springs
George Strube (for Sidney George Strube)
Daniel Topolski (for Feliks Topolski)
Rachael Whear (for David Low)

For the historical background, and detail about individuals the author has consulted a large number of books. These include, as well as individual biographies and autobiographies:

Blackwell Biographical Dictionary in the Twentieth Century, Edited by Keith Robbins, Blackwell 1990
Burke's Peerage and Baronetage
The Decline and Fall of the British Aristocracy, David Cannadine, Papermac 1996
Dictionary of Labour Biography Edited by G Rosen, Politicos 2001
Dictionary of Liberal Biography Edited by D Brack, Politicos 1998
Dictionary of National Biography
Dictionary of Twentieth Century British Cartoonists and Caricaturists, Mark Bryant, Ashgate 2000
Hope and Glory: Britain 1900–1990 Peter Clarke, Penguin 1997
The House of Lords, John Wells, Hodder and Stoughton 1997
Oxford Dictionary of Political Quotations, OUP 1999
Oxford Companion to Twentieth Century British Politics Edited by John Ramsden, OUP 2002